# Ninja Foodi Pressure Cooker and Air Fryer Cookbook

Holidays and Daily Diet Recipes to Air Fry, Broil, Pressure Cook, Slow Cook, Dehydrate, and More

(for Beginners and Advanced Users)

Christi Smith

# Table of Contents

# Introduction

The Ninja Foodi Multi-Crisp Cooker is nothing short of a revolutionary cooking appliance that has seemingly taken the whole culinary world by storm! The possibilities with this appliance are pretty much endless.

**It has the following characteristics and advantages:**

• The Ninja Foodi Deluxe—the deluxe pressure cooker that crisps. Deluxe cooking capacity - XL 8-quart pot, XL 5-quart Cook & Crisp Basket and Deluxe Reversible Rack let you cook for a small group.

• TenderCrisp Technology lets you quickly pressure cook ingredients to lock in juices, then give them a crispy, golden air-fryer finish. Deluxe Reversible Rack lets you steam and broil, as well as TenderCrisp up to 8 chicken breasts at once or add servings to layered 360 meals.

• XL 8-quart ceramic-coated pot: Nonstick, PTFE/PFOA free, and easy to hand-wash.

• XL 5-quart Cook & Crisp Basket: Large-capacity, ceramic-coated, PTFE/PFOA-free nonstick basket is dishwasher safe and holds up to a 7-lb. chicken to feed your whole family.

• 9 functions: Pressure Cook, Air Fry/Air Crisp, Steam, Slow Cook, Yogurt, Sear/Saute, Bake/Roast, Broil, Dehydrate

**Throughout the many absolutely amazing Ninja Foodi recipes found in this book, you will notice that I have tried to cover every single type of recipe possible. You will get easy to make recipes, meat, poultry, seafood, holiday recipes, and even simple 5 ingredient recipes, the list goes on!**

And if you are daring and want to take on more of a challenge, then a good number of slightly complicated recipes are also there to challenge your inner chef!

**Welcome, to the magic world of Ninja Foodi Cooking!**

# The Functions of Ninja Foodi

With the TenderCrisp tech out of the way, let me talk a little bit about the different buttons and features found in the Foodi. The following guide should help you understand what each of the buttons does and how you can use them to their fullest extent.

## Pressure

The Pressure Button will allow you to simply Pressure Cook your foods using the Ninja Foodi. This will allow you to cook meals almost 70% faster than other traditional methods. Releasing the pressure naturally is often recommended for tough meats while the quick release is often suited for tender cuts like fish or even vegetables.

## Bake/Roast

This particular function is for those who like to bake! The Bake/Roast function is an awesome mode that allows users to seamlessly use their Foodi as a regular oven (thanks to crisping lid) that allows them to create inspiring baked goods.

## Air Crisp

This is possibly the most unique feature of the Ninja Foodi. Using the Air Crisp feature, you will be able to use your Ninja Foodi as an Air Fryer, that allows you to add a nice crispy and crunchy texture with little to almost no oil. This particular setting cooks the food at extremely high temperatures of 300F to 400F.

## Steam

This particular button allows you to use the "Steam" function of the Ninja Foodi. Using steam, you will be able to cook very delicate food at high temperatures. Just make sure to use at least a cup of liquid when steaming your food. While using this feature, make sure to use the Pressure Lid.

## Slow Cooker

This particular button will allow you to utilize the Slow Cooker mode that allows you to use the Ninja Foodi as a traditional Slow Cooker. Through this method, your cooks will be cooked at a very low temperature over a prolonged period of time. The time can be adjusted from 12-4 hours, and once the cooking is done, the appliance will automatically switch to "KEEP WARM" function where the meal stays hot until you open it up.

## Sear/Saute

This particular button allows you to use your Ninja Foodi to brown meat. This feature is excellent when you need searing or browning meat/ Sautéing spices. This same function can also be used to simmer sauces. Similar to Broil mode, this does not come with a temperature setting, rather, once you are done browning, you simply need to press the "START/STOP" button to initiate or stop the process.

## Broil

The Broil feature is used in conjunction with the Crisping Lid in order to slightly brown or caramelizes the surface of your food. It cooks food at a higher temperature to create the required brown surface.

## Dehydrate

The Dehydrate function allows you to dehydrate food between 105 degrees F and 195 degrees F, and this feature will allow you to make healthy dried snacks out of meat, vegetables, and fruits. However, if you want to use this device, it is advised that you purchase a dehydrating rack for maximum efficiency.

# Important Tips to Using Ninja Foodi

As time goes on, you will learn how to utilize the power of your Ninja Foodi to its full extent. However, the following tips will help you during the early days of your life with the Foodi and ensure that your experience is as pleasant and smooth as possible.

• It is crucial that you don't just press the function buttons randomly! Try to read through the function of each button and use them according to the requirement of your recipe.

• It is important that you place the lid properly while closing the appliance as it greatly affects the cooking. Therefore, make sure that your lid is tightly close by ensuring that the silicone ring inside the lid is placed all the way around the groove.

• This is something that many people don't know, once the cooking timer of your appliance hits '0', the pot will automatically go into "Natural Pressure Release" mode where it will start to release the pressure on its own. You can use a quick release anytime to release all the steam at once, or you can wait for 10-15 minutes until the steam vents off.

• If you are in a rush and want to release the pressure quickly, turn the pressure valve to "Open Position," which will quick release all the pressure. But this can be a little risky as a lot of steam comes out at once, so be sure to stay careful.

• If you are dealing with a recipe that calls for unfrozen meat, make sure to use the same amount of cooking time and liquid that you would use if you were to use frozen meat of the same type.

• Once you start using the appliance for cooking, make sure to check if the Pressure Valve is in the "Locked Position." If it is not, your appliance won't be able to build up pressure inside for cooking.

• Make sure to keep in mind that the "Timer" button isn't a button to set time! Rather it acts as a Delay Timer. Using this button, you will be able to set a specific time, after which the Ninja Foodi will automatically wake up and start cooking the food.

# Chapter 1: Breakfast Recipes

## Soft Eggs

(Prepping time: 4 minutes| Cooking Time: 4 minutes |Serves: 3)

**Ingredients:**

- 3 eggs
- 6 ounces ham
- 1 teaspoon salt
- ½ teaspoon ground white pepper
- 1 teaspoon paprika
- ¼ teaspoon ground ginger
- 2 tablespoons chives

**Preparation:**

Take three small ramekins and coat them with vegetable oil spray. Beat the eggs add an equal amount to the ramekins. Sprinkle the eggs with the salt, ground black pepper, and paprika. Transfer the ramekins to the pressure cooker and set the mode to "Steam." Close the lid, and cook for 4 minutes. Meanwhile, chop the ham and chives and combine them. Add ground ginger and stir into the ham mixture well. Transfer the mixture to the serving plates. When the cooking time ends, remove the eggs from the pressure cooker and put them atop the ham mixture.

**Nutritional Information Per Serving:**

calories 205, fat 11.1, fiber 1, carbs 6.47, protein 19

## Aromatic Keto Coffee

(Prepping time: 10 minutes| Cooking Time: 5 minutes |Serves: 4)

**Ingredients:**

- 4 teaspoon butter
- 2 cups of water
- 4 teaspoons instant coffee
- 1 tablespoon Erythritol
- 1/3 cup heavy cream
- 1 teaspoon ground cinnamon
- ½ teaspoon vanilla extract

**Preparation:**

1. Pour water, heavy cream, ground cinnamon, and vanilla extract in the cooker. Add instant coffee and stir well until homogenous. Close and seal the lid. Cook the coffee mixture on high-pressure mode for 4 minutes. Then allow natural pressure release for 10 minutes.

2. Open the lid and add butter. Stir well and pour coffee in the serving cups.

**Nutritional Information Per Serving:**

calories 71, fat 7.5, fiber 0.3, carbs 0.8, protein 0.3

# Cauliflower Pancake

(Prepping time: 10 minutes| Cooking Time: 10 minutes |Serves: 2)

**Ingredients:**

- 7 oz cauliflower
- 2 eggs, whisked
- 2 tablespoons almond flour
- 1 tablespoon flax meal
- 1 teaspoon butter
- 1 teaspoon chili flakes
- 1 teaspoon dried dill

**Preparation:**

Grind the cauliflower and mix it up with the whisked eggs, almond flour, flax meal, chili flakes, and dried dill. Stir the mixture well. Preheat Ninja cooker on saute mode and add butter. Melt it. Place cauliflower mixture in the cooker with the help of the spoon (to get pancake shape) and cook for 4 minutes from each side.

**Nutritional Information Per Serving:**

calories 161, fat 11.2, fiber 4.3, carbs 8.4, protein 9.9

# Zucchini Egg Cups

(Prepping time: 5 minutes| Cooking Time: 7 minutes |Serves: 4)

**Ingredients:**

- 1 zucchini
- 2 tablespoon almond flour
- ½ teaspoon salt
- 1 teaspoon butter
- 4 eggs

**Preparation:**

Grate zucchini and mix it up with almond flour and salt. Spread the muffin molds with butter and place grated zucchini inside in the shape of nests. Then beat eggs inside "zucchini nests" and place them in the cooker. Lower the air fryer lid. Cook the zucchini cups for 7 minutes. When the eggs are solid, the meal is cooked.

**Nutritional Information Per Serving:**

calories 99, fat 7.2, fiber 0.9, carbs 2.7, protein 6.9

# Bacon Eggs

(Prepping time: 7 minutes| Cooking Time: 7 minutes |Serves: 4)

## Ingredients:

- 7 ounces sliced bacon
- 4 eggs, boiled
- 1 teaspoon cilantro
- ½ cup spinach
- 2 teaspoons butter
- ½ teaspoon ground white pepper
- 3 tablespoons heavy cream

## Preparation:

Lay the bacon flat and sprinkle it with the ground white pepper and cilantro on both sides of the slices and stir the mixture. Peel the eggs, and wrap them in the spinach leaves. Wrap the eggs in the sliced bacon. Set the pressure cooker mode to "Sauté" and transfer the wrapped eggs. Add butter and cook for 10 minutes. When the cooking time ends, remove the eggs from the pressure cooker and sprinkle them with the cream. Serve the dish immediately.

## Nutritional Information Per Serving:

calories 325, fat 28.4, fiber 2, carbs 5.24, protein 15

# Egg Clouds

(Prepping time: 10 minutes| Cooking Time: 6 minutes |Serves: 4)

## Ingredients:

- 4 egg whites
- ½ teaspoon lemon juice
- ½ teaspoon salt
- 1 teaspoon almond flour

## Preparation:

Whisk the egg whites with lemon juice until strong peaks. Add salt and almond flour. Stir it. Place the egg white clouds in the cooker with the help of the spoon. Lower the air fryer lid. Cook the egg clouds for 6 minutes or until they are light brown.

## Nutritional Information Per Serving:

calories 21, fat 0.4, fiber 0.1, carbs 0.4, protein 3.7

# Baked Avocado

(Prepping time: 15 minutes| Cooking Time: 10 minutes |Serves: 2)

**Ingredients:**

- 1 avocado, halved
- 2 eggs
- ½ teaspoon ground black pepper
- 1 teaspoon butter

**Preparation:**

Beat the eggs in the avocado halves, sprinkle with ground black pepper. Then add butter. Add 1 cup of water in the cooker. Transfer the avocado halves on the trivet in the Ninja Pressure cooker and close the lid. Cook the breakfast for 10 minutes on High-pressure mode. Then allow natural pressure release for 10 minutes.

**Nutritional Information Per Serving:**

calories 286, fat 25.2, fiber 6.9, carbs 9.3, protein 7.5

# Creamy Pumpkin Slow Cook

(Prepping time: 10 minutes| Cooking Time: 15 minutes |Serves: 5)

**Ingredients:**

- 1 cup almond milk
- 1 cup of water
- 1 pound pumpkin
- 1 teaspoon cinnamon
- ½ teaspoon cardamom
- ½ teaspoon turmeric
- ⅓ cup coconut flakes
- 2 teaspoons Erythritol

**Preparation:**

Peel the pumpkin and chop it roughly. Transfer the chopped pumpkin in the pressure cooker and add almond milk and water. Sprinkle the mixture with the cinnamon, cardamom, turmeric, and Erythritol. Add coconut flakes and stir the mixture well. Close the pressure cooker lid, and set the mode to "Sauté." Cook for 15 minutes. When the cooking time ends, blend the mixture until smooth using a hand blender. Ladle the pumpkin Slow Cook in the serving bowls and serve.

**Nutritional Information Per Serving:**

calories 163, fat 13.5, fiber 4.5, carbs 13.1, protein 2.3

# Stuffed Buns with Egg

(Prepping time: 8 minutes| Cooking Time: 10 minutes |Serves: 6)

**Ingredients:**

- 3 large keto bread rolls
- 4 eggs
- 7 ounces cheddar cheese
- 1 teaspoon salt
- ½ teaspoon red chili flakes
- ½ teaspoon sour cream
- 1 tablespoon butter

**Preparation:**

Cut the keto bread rolls in half. Hollow out the center of the bread half partially. Combine the salt, pepper flakes, and sour cream together and stir gently. Add the eggs to a mixing bowl and whisk. Add the butter in the pressure cooker. Pour the eggs equally into the keto bread roll halves. Transfer the bread in the pressure cooker. Sprinkle the dish with the spice mixture. Grate the cheddar cheese and sprinkle the bread with the grated cheese. Close the lid, and set the pressure cooker mode to "Steam." Cook for 10 minutes. Let the dish rest before serving it.

**Nutritional Information Per Serving:**

calories 259, fat 19.2, fiber 3.6, carbs 2.6, protein 17.5

# Chicken Breakfast Burrito

(Prepping time: 10 minutes| Cooking Time: 45 minutes |Serves: 6)

**Ingredients:**

- 6 large almond flour tortillas (keto tortillas)
- 1 pound chicken
- ½ cup chicken stock
- 1 tablespoon tomato paste
- 1 teaspoon sour cream
- 1 teaspoon ground black pepper
- ½ teaspoon paprika
- 1 teaspoon cilantro
- ½ teaspoon turmeric
- 1 white onion
- 2 sweet bell peppers
- ½ cup cauliflower rice
- 1 cup of water

**Preparation:**

Chop the chicken roughly and transfer it to the pressure cooker. Add chicken stock, tomato paste, sour cream, and water. Sprinkle the mixture with the ground black pepper, paprika, cilantro, and turmeric. Peel the onion, and remove the seeds from the bell peppers. Dice onion and peppers and set aside. Sprinkle the pressure cooker mixture with the cauliflower rice and close the lid. Set the pressure cooker mode to "Steam," and cook for 30 minutes. Add the chopped onion and peppers and cook for 15 minutes. When the cooking time ends, shred the chicken and transfer the mixture to the tortillas. Wrap the tortillas and serve the dish immediately.

**Nutritional Information Per Serving:**

calories 295, fat 10.8, fiber 5.2, carbs 14.3, protein 35.1

# Milky Tomato Omelet

(Prepping time: 8 minutes| Cooking Time: 9 minutes |Serves: 6)

**Ingredients:**

- 5 eggs
- ½ cup of coconut milk
- 4 tablespoons tomato paste
- 1 teaspoon salt
- 1 tablespoon turmeric
- ½ cup cilantro
- 1 tablespoon butter
- 4 ounces Parmesan cheese

**Preparation:**

Whisk the eggs with the coconut milk and tomato paste in the mixing bowl. Add salt and turmeric and stir the mixture. Grate the Parmesan cheese and add it to the egg mixture. Mince the cilantro and add it to the egg mixture. Add the butter in the pressure cooker and pour in the egg mixture. Close the pressure cooker lid, and set the mode to "Steam." Cook for 9 minutes. Open the pressure cooker to let the omelet rest. Transfer it to serving plates and enjoy.

**Nutritional Information Per Serving:**

calories 189, fat 14.6, fiber 1.2, carbs 4.9, protein 11.7

# Zucchini Quiche

(Prepping time: 15 minutes| Cooking Time: 40 minutes |Serves: 6)

**Ingredients:**

- 3 green zucchini
- 7 ounces puff pastry
- 2 onions
- 1 cup dill

- 2 eggs
- 3 tablespoons butter
- ½ cup cream
- 6 ounces cheddar cheese
- 1 teaspoon salt
- 1 teaspoon paprika

**Preparation:**

Wash the zucchini and grate the vegetables. Peel the onions and chop them. Grate the cheddar cheese. Whisk the eggs in the mixing bowl. Roll out the puff pastry. Spread the pressure cooker basket with the butter and transfer the dough to there. Add grated zucchini and chopped onions, and sprinkle the vegetable mixture with the salt and paprika. Chop the dill and add it to the quiche. Sprinkle the dish with the grated cheese and egg mixture, and pour the cream on top. Close the pressure cooker lid, and set the mode to "Steam." Cook the quiche for 40 minutes. When the cooking time ends, check if the dish is cooked and remove it from the pressure cooker. Let the dish cool briefly and serve.

**Nutritional Information Per Serving:**

calories 398, fat 28.4, fiber 2, carbs 25.82, protein 12

# Creamy Soufflé

(Prepping time: 10 minutes| Cooking Time: 20 minutes |Serves: 6)

**Ingredients:**

- 3 eggs
- 1 cup cream
- 6 ounces of cottage cheese
- 4 tablespoons butter
- ⅓ cup dried apricots
- 1 tablespoon sour cream
- 2 tablespoons sugar
- 1 teaspoon vanilla extract

**Preparation:**

Whisk the eggs and combine them with cream. Transfer the cottage cheese to a mixing bowl, and mix it well using a hand mixer. Add the whisked eggs, butter, sour cream, sugar, and vanilla extract. Blend the mixture well until smooth. Add the apricots, and stir the mixture well. Transfer the soufflé in the pressure cooker and close the lid. Set the pressure cooker mode to «Sauté», and cook for 20 minutes. When the cooking time ends, let the soufflé cool little and serve.

**Nutritional Information Per Serving:**

calories 266, fat 21.1, fiber 1, carbs 11.72, protein 8

# Spicy Bacon Bites

(Prepping time: 6 minutes| Cooking Time: 20 minutes |Serves: 8)

**Ingredients:**

- 10 ounces Romano cheese
- 6 ounces sliced bacon
- 1 teaspoon oregano
- 5 ounces puff pastry
- 1 teaspoon butter
- 2 egg yolks
- 1 teaspoon sesame seeds

**Preparation:**

Chop Romano cheese into small cubes. Roll the puff pastry using a rolling pin. Whisk the egg yolks. Sprinkle them with the oregano and sesame seeds. Cut the puff pastry into the squares, and place an equal amount of butter on every square. Wrap the cheese cubes in the sliced bacon. Place the wrapped cheese cubes onto the puff pastry squares. Make the "bites" of the dough and brush them with the egg yolk mixture. Transfer the bites in the pressure cooker. Close the lid, and set the pressure cooker mode to "Steam." Cook for 20 minutes. When the cooking time ends, remove the dish from the pressure cooker and place on a serving dish.

**Nutritional Information Per Serving:**

calories 321, fat 24.4, fiber 1, carbs 10.9, protein 16

# Avocado Bacon Bombs

(Prepping time: 10 minutes| Cooking Time: 10 minutes |Serves: 4)

**Ingredients:**

- 1 avocado, peeled, cored
- 4 oz bacon, sliced
- 1 tablespoon almond flour
- 1 tablespoon flax meal
- ½ teaspoon salt

**Preparation:**

Blend together avocado, almond flour, flax meal, and salt. When the mixture is smooth, transfer it in the mixing bowl. Make the medium size balls from it and wrap in the bacon. Secure the balls with the toothpicks. After this, transfer the bombs in the cooker and ser air crisp mode. Close the lid and cook the meal for 10 minutes.

**Nutritional Information Per Serving:**

calories 303, fat 25.8, fiber 4.6, carbs 6.7, protein 13.3

# Poached Tomato Eggs

(Prepping time: 5 minutes| Cooking Time: 5 minutes |Serves: 4)

## Ingredients:

- 4 eggs
- 3 medium tomatoes
- 1 red onion
- 1 teaspoon salt
- 1 tablespoon olive oil
- ½ teaspoon white pepper
- ½ teaspoon paprika
- 1 tablespoon fresh dill

## Preparation:

Spray the ramekins with the olive oil inside. Beat the eggs in a mixing bowl and add an equal amount to each ramekin. Combine the paprika, white pepper, fresh dill, and salt together in a mixing bowl and stir the mixture. Dice the red onion and tomatoes and combine. Add the seasonings and stir the mixture. Sprinkle the eggs with the tomato mixture. Transfer the eggs to the pressure cooker. Close the lid, and set the pressure cooker mode to "Steam". Cook for 5 minutes. Remove the dish from the pressure cooker and rest briefly. Let it rest for a few minutes and dish immediately.

## Nutritional Information Per Serving:

calories 194, fat 13.5, fiber 2, carbs 8.45, protein 10

# Mason Jar Omelet

(Prepping time: 10 minutes| Cooking Time: 7 minutes |Serves: 4)

## Ingredients:

- 4 eggs, whisked
- ¼ cup cream
- ½ teaspoon salt
- 2 oz bacon, chopped
- 1 teaspoon butter, melted
- 1 cup water, for cooking

## Preparation:

Mix up together whisked eggs, cream, salt, and chopped bacon. Add melted butter and stir the mixture. Pour egg mixture in the mason jars. Pour 1 cup of water in the Pressure cooker and insert trivet. Place mason jars on the trivet. Close the lid and cook an omelet for 7 minutes on High-pressure mode. Then use quick pressure release. Chill the meal little before serving.

## Nutritional Information Per Serving:

calories 234, fat 18, fiber 0, carbs 1.2, protein 16.2

# Scrambled Eggs

(Prepping time: 5 minutes| Cooking Time: 9 minutes |Serves: 5)

**Ingredients:**

- 7 eggs
- ½ cup almond milk
- 1 tablespoon butter
- 1 teaspoon basil
- ¼ cup fresh parsley
- 1 teaspoon salt
- 1 teaspoon paprika
- 4 ounces sliced bacon
- 1 tablespoon cilantro

**Preparation:**

Beat the eggs in a mixing bowl and whisk well. Add the almond milk, basil, salt, paprika, and cilantro. Stir the mixture well. Chop the bacon and parsley. Set the pressure cooker mode to "Sauté" and add the bacon. Cook it for 3 minutes. Add the whisked egg mixture, and cook for 5 additional minutes. Stir the eggs carefully using a wooden spoon or spatula. Sprinkle the eggs with the chopped parsley, and cook it for 4 minutes. When the eggs are cooked, remove them from the pressure cooker.

**Nutritional Information Per Serving:**

calories 289, fat 23.7, fiber 0.8, carbs 2.6, protein 16.9

# Spinach Egg Omelet

(Prepping time: 6 minutes| Cooking Time: 6 minutes |Serves: 5)

**Ingredients:**

- 2 cups spinach
- 8 eggs
- ½ cup almond milk
- 1 teaspoon salt
- 1 tablespoon olive oil
- 1 teaspoon ground black pepper
- 4 ounces Parmesan cheese

**Preparation:**

Add the eggs to a mixing bowl and whisk them. Chop the spinach and add it to the egg mixture. Add the almond milk, salt, olive oil, and ground black pepper. Stir the mixture well. Transfer the egg mixture to the pressure cooker and close the lid. Set the pressure cooker mode to "Steam," and cook for 6 minutes. Grate the cheese. When the cooking time ends, remove the omelet from the pressure cooker and transfer it to a serving plate. Sprinkle the dish with the grated cheese and serve.

# Migas

(Prepping time: 10 minutes| Cooking Time: 10 minutes |Serves: 6)

## Ingredients:

- 10 eggs
- 1 jalapeno pepper
- 8 ounces tomatoes
- 1 tablespoon chicken stock
- 7 ounces cheddar cheese
- 2 white onions
- 2 cups tortilla chips
- 1 sweet bell pepper
- ½ cup beef stock
- 1 teaspoon salt

## Preparation:

Whisk the eggs in the mixing bowl. Chop the jalapeno peppers and tomatoes. Grate the cheddar cheese. Peel the onions and chop them. Crush the tortilla chips. Chop the bell peppers. Combine the jalapeno pepper, tomatoes, onion, and chopped bell pepper together and stir the mixture. Set the pressure cooker mode to "Sauté", and transfer the vegetable mixture. Cook it for 5 minutes. Add the whisked eggs mixture. Add the stocks, salt, and grated cheese. Mix up the mixture well, and cook it for 4 minutes. Add the crushed tortilla chips, and cook for 1 minute more. Stir it and serve. Note: Only add salt if using low-sodium chicken and beef stock; otherwise, you can omit the salt.!

## Nutritional Information Per Serving:

calories 295, fat 19.3, fiber 1, carbs 9.27, protein 21

# Soft-boiled Eggs

(Prepping time: 15 minutes| Cooking Time: 15 minutes |Serves: 6)

**Ingredients:**

- 2 cups of water
- 1 avocado, pitted
- 4 eggs
- 1 teaspoon paprika
- ½ teaspoon ground black pepper
- 1 sweet bell pepper
- 1 teaspoon salt
- 3 tablespoons heavy cream
- 3 ounces lettuce leaves

**Preparation:**

Put the eggs and water in the pressure cooker and close the lid. Set the pressure cooker mode to "Pressure," and cook for 15 minutes. Remove the eggs from the pressure cooker, and transfer them to an ice bath. Chop the avocado, and remove the seeds from bell pepper. Dice the bell peppers and Peel the eggs and chop them. Combine the chopped ingredients together in a mixing bowl. Sprinkle the mixture with the paprika, ground black pepper, salt, and stir. Transfer the mixture in the lettuce leaves, sprinkle them with the cream, and serve.

**Nutritional Information Per Serving:**

calories 168, fat 12.9, fiber 3, carbs 6.75, protein 7

# Chapter 2: Beef and Pork Recipes

## Southern-Style Lettuce Wraps

(Prepping time: 10 minutes| Cooking Time: 30 minutes |Serves: 6)

**Ingredients:**

- 3 pounds boneless pork shoulder, cut into 1- to 2-inch cubes
- 2 cups light beer
- 1 cup brown sugar
- 1 teaspoon chipotle chiles in adobo sauce
- 1 cup barbecue sauce
- 1 head iceberg lettuce, quartered and leaves separated
- 1 cup roasted peanuts, chopped or ground
- Cilantro leaves

**Preparation:**

1. Place the pork, beer, brown sugar, chipotle, and barbecue sauce in the pot. Assemble pressure lid, making sure the pressure release valve is in the seal position.

2. Select pressure and set to HI. Set the timer to 30 minutes. Select start/stop to begin.

3. When pressure cooking is complete, quick release the pressure by turning the pressure release valve to the vent position. Carefully remove lid when unit has finished releasing pressure.

4. Using a silicone-tipped utensil, shred the pork in the pot. Stir to mix the meat in with the sauce.

5. Place a small amount of pork in a piece of lettuce. Top with peanuts and cilantro to serve.

**Nutritional Information Per Serving:**

Calories: 811, Fats 58g, Carbs: 22g, Protein: 45g


## Beef Cooked in Mango-Turmeric Spice

(Prepping time: 4 minutes| Cooking Time: 50 minutes |Serves: 2)

**Ingredients:**

- 1-pound beef shin, cut into chunks
- ½ teaspoon ground cinnamon
- ¼ teaspoon ground cloves
- 1 teaspoon dried mango powder
- 1 teaspoon ground turmeric
- ½ teaspoon ground cumin
- 3 cloves of garlic, minced
- 1 tablespoon lemon juice

- 1 teaspoon honey
- 12 cardamom pods, bashed
- Salt and pepper to taste
- 2 tablespoons ghee
- 1 cup onions, cut into wedges
- 2 green chilies, sliced
- 2 tomatoes, chopped
- 1 cup water

**Preparation:**

1. In a mixing bowl, combine the first 11 ingredients and allow to marinate in the fridge for at least 2 hours.

2. Press the sauté button on the Ninja Foodi and add the ghee. Stir in the marinated beef and sear button on all sides for at least 5 minutes.

3. Stir in the rest of the ingredients.

4. Install pressure lid. Close Ninja Foodi, press the pressure button, choose high settings, and set time to 45 minutes.

5. Once done cooking, do a quick release.

6. Serve and enjoy.

**Nutritional Information Per Serving:**

Calories 463; carbohydrates: 19.3g; protein: 51.5g; fat: 20g

# Bacon-Wrapped Hot Dogs

(Prepping time: 15 minutes| Cooking Time: 15 minutes |Serves: 3)

**Ingredients:**
- 4 beef hot dogs
- 4 bacon strips
- Cooking spray
- 4 bakery hot dog buns, split and toasted
- ½ red onion, chopped
- 1 cup sauerkraut, rinsed and drained

**Preparation:**

1. Place Cook & Crisp Basket in pot. Close crisping lid. Select AIR CRISP, set temperature to 360°F, and set time to 5 minutes. Select START/STOP to begin preheating.

2. Wrap each hot dog with 1 strip of bacon, securing it with toothpicks as needed.

3. Once unit has preheated, open lid and coat the basket with cooking spray. Place the hot dogs in the basket in a single layer. Close crisping lid.

4.  Select AIR CRISP, set temperature to 360°F, and set time to 15 minutes. Select START/STOP to begin.

5.  After 10 minutes, open lid and check doneness. If needed, continue cooking until it reaches your desired doneness.

6.  When cooking is complete, place the hot dog in the buns with the onion and sauerkraut. Top, if desired, with condiments of your choice, such as yellow mustard, ketchup, or mayonnaise.

**Nutritional Information Per Serving:**

Calories: 336; Fat: 17g; Carbohydrates: 27g; Protein: 20g

# Perfect Sichuan Pork Soup

(Prepping time: 10 minutes| Cooking Time: 20 minutes |Serves: 6)

**Ingredients:**

*   2 tablespoons olive oil
*   1 tablespoon garlic, minced
*   1 tablespoon fresh ginger, minced
*   2 tablespoons coconut aminos
*   2 tablespoons black vinegar
*   1-2 teaspoons stevia
*   1-2 teaspoons salt
*   ½ onion, sliced
*   1-pound pork shoulder, cut into 2-inch chunks
*   2 pepper corns, crushed
*   3 cups water
*   3-4 cups bok choy, chopped
*   ¼ cup fresh cilantro, chopped

**Preparation:**

1.  Pre-heat your Ninja Foodi by setting it to Saute mode on HIGH settings
2.  Once the inner pot it hot enough, add oil and let heat until shimmering
3.  Add garlic and ginger and Saute for 1-2 minutes
4.  Add coconut aminos, vinegar, sweetener, pepper corn, salt, onion, pork, water and stir
5.  Lock lid and cook on high pressure for 20 minutes
6.  Release pressure naturally over 10 minutes
7.  Open lid and add bok choy, close lid and let it cook in the remaining heat for 10 minutes
8.  Ladle soup into serving bowl and serve with topping of cilantro
9.  Enjoy!

**Nutritional Information Per Serving:**

Calories: 256, Fat: 20g, Carbs: 5g, Protein: 14g

# Beef Pot Pie

(Prepping time: 6 minutes| Cooking Time: 25 minutes |Serves: 2)

**Ingredients:**

- 1 ½ tablespoons butter
- ½ cup diced onion
- ½ cup diced celery
- 2 cloves of garlic, minced
- 6-oz beef
- 1 teaspoon dried thyme
- ¾ cup potatoes, diced
- 1/3 cup carrots, diced
- 1/3 cup frozen peas
- ¾ cups beef broth
- 2 tbsp milk
- 1 tablespoon cornstarch + 1 ½ tablespoons water
- ½ box puff pastry
- 1 egg white

**Preparation:**

1. Press the sauté button on the Ninja Foodi and heat the butter. Sauté the onion, celery and garlic until fragrant. Add the beef and sear button for 5 minutes.

2. Stir in the thyme, potatoes, carrots, frozen peas, beef broth and milk.

3. Install pressure lid. Close Ninja Foodi, press pressure button, choose high settings, and set time to 10 minutes.

4. Once done cooking, do a quick release.

5. Ladle into two ramekins and cover the top of the ramekins with puff pastry. Brush the top with egg whites.

6. Place in Ninja Foodi, bake at 3500F for 10 minutes or until tops are lightly browned.

**Nutritional Information Per Serving:**

Calories 328; carbohydrates: 26.6g; protein: 20.8g; fat: 15.3g

# Broccoli Pork with Rice

(Prepping time: 5 minutes| Cooking Time: 14 minutes |Serves: 4)

**Ingredients:**

- 1 head broccoli, cut into florets
- 1 tablespoon extra-virgin olive oil
- ¼ teaspoon black pepper

- ¼ teaspoon sea salt
- 1 cup long-grain white rice
- 1 cup water
- 1 trimmed pork tenderloin, cut into 1-inch pieces
- 1 cup teriyaki sauce
- Sesame seeds to garnish

**Preparation:**

1.  In a mixing bowl, combine the broccoli with the olive oil. Season with the ground black pepper and salt.

2.  In another bowl, combine the sauce and pork until evenly coated.

3.  Take Ninja Foodi multi-cooker, arrange it over a cooking platform, and open the top lid.

4.  In the pot, add the water and rice.

5.  Seal the multi-cooker by locking it with the pressure lid; ensure to keep the pressure release valve locked/sealed.

6.  Select "pressure" mode and select the "HI" pressure level. Then, set timer to 2 minutes and press "stop/start"; it will start the cooking process by building up inside pressure.

7.  When the timer goes off, quick release pressure by adjusting the pressure valve to the vent. After pressure gets released, open the pressure lid.

8.  Over the rice, arrange the reversible rack and place the pork and broccoli over the rack.

9.  Seal the multi-cooker by locking it with the crisping lid; ensure to keep the pressure release valve locked/sealed.

10.  Select "broil" mode and select the "HI" pressure level. Then, set timer to 12 minutes and press "stop/start"; it will start the cooking process by building up inside pressure.

11.  When the timer goes off, quick release pressure by adjusting the pressure valve to the vent.

12.  After pressure gets released, open the pressure lid.

13.  Serve the pork mixture warm with the cooked rice and some sesame seeds on top.

**Nutritional Information Per Serving:**

Calories: 453, Fats 9.5g, Carbs: 52g, Protein: 39g

# Delightful Cheese Casserole

(Prepping time: 10 minutes| Cooking Time: 30 minutes |Serves: 8)

**Ingredients:**

- 6 ounces cheddar cheese
- 1 zucchini
- ½ cup ground chicken
- 4 ounces Parmesan cheese
- 3 tablespoons butter

- 1 teaspoon paprika
- 1 teaspoon salt
- 1 teaspoon basil
- 1 teaspoon cilantro
- ½ cup fresh dill
- ⅓ cup tomato juice
- ½ cup cream
- 2 red sweet bell peppers

**Preparation:**

Grate cheddar cheese. Chop the zucchini and combine it with the ground chicken. Sprinkle the mixture with the paprika, salt, basil, cilantro, tomato juice, and cream. Stir the mixture well. Transfer it to the pressure cooker. Chop the dill, sprinkle the mixture in the pressure cooker, and add the butter. Chop the Parmesan cheese and add it to the pressure cooker. Chop the bell peppers and add them too. Sprinkle the mixture with the grated cheddar cheese and close the lid. Set the pressure cooker mode to "Sauté", and cook for 30 minutes. When the cooking time ends, let the casserole chill briefly and serve.

**Nutritional Information Per Serving:**

calories 199, fat 14.7, fiber 1, carbs 6.55, protein 11

# Beefy Stew Recipe from Persia

(Prepping time: 6 minutes| Cooking Time: 20 minutes |Serves: 2)

**Ingredients:**
- 1 tablespoons vegetable oil
- 1 onion, chopped
- 2 cloves of garlic, minced
- ¾-pound beef stew meat, cut into chunks
- ½ tablespoon ground cumin
- ¼ teaspoon saffron threads
- ½ teaspoon turmeric
- ¼ teaspoon ground cinnamon
- ¼ teaspoon ground allspice
- Salt and pepper to taste
- 2 tbsp tomato paste
- ½ can split peas, rinsed and drained
- 2 cups bone broth
- 1 can crushed tomatoes
- 2 tablespoon lemon juice, freshly squeezed

**Preparation:**

1. Press the sauté button on the Ninja Foodi. Heat the oil and sauté the onion and garlic until fragrant. Add cumin, saffron, turmeric, cinnamon, and allspice. Stir in the beef and sear button for 3 minutes. Season with salt and pepper to taste.

2. Pour in the rest of the ingredients.

3. Install pressure lid. Close Ninja Foodi, press the pressure button, choose high settings, and set time to 20 minutes.

4. Once done cooking, do a quick release.

**Nutritional Information Per Serving:**

Calories 466; carbohydrates: 36g; protein: 49g; fat: 14g

# Mustard Dredged Pork Chops

(Prepping time: 10 minutes| Cooking Time: 30 minutes |Serves: 4)

**Ingredients:**

- 2 tablespoons butter
- 2 tablespoons Dijon mustard
- 4 pork chops
- Salt and pepper to taste
- 1 tablespoon fresh rosemary, coarsely chopped

**Preparation:**

1. Take a bowl and add pork chops, cover with Dijon mustard and carefully sprinkle rosemary, salt and pepper

2. Let it marinate for 2 hours

3. Add butter and marinated pork chops to your Ninja Foodi pot

4. Lock lid and cook on Low-Medium Pressure for 30 minutes

5. Release pressure naturally over 10 minutes

6. Take the dish out, serve and enjoy!

**Nutritional Information Per Serving:**

Calories: 315, Fat: 26g, Carbs:1g Protein: 18g

# Classic Pork Meal with Green Bean

(Prepping time: 5 minutes| Cooking Time: 25 minutes |Serves: 4)

**Ingredients:**

- 2 pounds pork stew meat, cut into small cubes
- 1 tablespoon avocado oil
- 1-pound green beans, trimmed and halved
- 2 minced garlic cloves

- 1 tablespoon basil, chopped
- 1 teaspoon chili powder
- ¾ cup veggie stock
- A pinch of black pepper and salt

**Preparation:**

1. Take Ninja Foodi multi-cooker, arrange it over a cooking platform, and open the top lid.

2. In the pot, add the oil; Select "sear/sauté" mode and select "md: hi" pressure level.

3. Press "stop/start." After about 4-5 minutes, the oil will start simmering.

4. Add the meat, garlic, and stir-cook for about 4-5 minutes to brown evenly.

5. Add the remaining ingredients; stir well.

6. Seal the multi-cooker by locking it with the pressure lid; ensure to keep the pressure release valve locked/sealed.

7. Select "pressure" mode and select the "HI" pressure level. Then, set timer to 20 minutes and press "stop/start"; it will start the cooking process by building up inside pressure.

8. When the timer goes off, naturally release inside pressure for about 8-10 minutes. Then, quick-release pressure by adjusting the pressure valve to the vent.

9. After pressure gets released, open the pressure lid.

10. Serve warm.

**Nutritional Information Per Serving:**

Calories: 403, Fat: 15.5g, Carbs: 18g, Protein: 53.5g

# Beef 'n Mushrooms in Thick Sauce

(Prepping time: 5 minutes| Cooking Time: 30 minutes |Serves: 2)

**Ingredients:**

- ½ tablespoon butter
- ½ pound beef chunks
- Salt and pepper to taste
- ½ cup onions, chopped
- ½ tablespoon garlic, minced
- 1 carrot, sliced diagonally
- ¼ cup chopped celery
- 1/3 cup mushrooms, halved
- 1 medium potato, peeled and quartered
- 1 tablespoon Worcestershire sauce
- 1 tablespoon tomato paste
- ½ cup chicken broth
- 1 tablespoon all-purpose flour + 1 tablespoon water

**Preparation:**

1.  Turn on the sauté button on the Ninja Foodi and melt the butter. Sear button the beef chunks and season with salt and pepper to taste. Add the onions and garlic until fragrant.

2.  Stir in the carrots, celery, mushrooms and potatoes.

3.  Add the Worcestershire sauce, tomato paste, and chicken broth. Season with more salt and pepper to taste.

4.  Install pressure lid. Close Ninja Foodi, press the pressure button, choose high settings, and set time to 30 minutes.

5.  Once done cooking, do a quick release.

6.  Open the lid and press the sauté button. Stir in the all-purpose flour and allow to simmer until the sauce thickens.

7.  Serve and enjoy.

**Nutritional Information Per Serving:**

Calories 539; carbohydrates: 61.3g; protein 43.9g, fat: 13.1g

# Healthy 'n Tasty Meatloaf

(Prepping time: 7 minutes| Cooking Time: 20 minutes |Serves: 2)

**Ingredients:**

*   ¾-pound ground beef
*   ¾ cup bread crumbs
*   1/3 cup parmesan cheese
*   2 small eggs, beaten
*   1 tablespoon minced garlic
*   1 teaspoon steak seasoning
*   Salt and pepper to taste
*   1 ½ teaspoons sear button sugar
*   ¼ cup ketchup
*   ½ tablespoon mustard
*   1 teaspoon Worcestershire sauce

**Preparation:**

1.  Place a trivet in the Ninja Foodi and pour a cup of beef broth.

2.  In a mixing bowl, mix together the beef, bread crumbs, cheese, eggs, garlic, and steak seasoning. Season with salt and pepper to taste.

3.  Pour meat mixture in a heat-proof pan and place on top of the trivet. Cover top with foil.

4.  Install pressure lid. Close Ninja Foodi, press the steam button, and set time to 20 minutes.

5.  While waiting for the meatloaf to cook, combine in a saucepan the sugar, ketchup, mustard, and Worcestershire sauce. Mix until the sauce becomes thick.

6. Once done cooking, do a quick release.

7. Remove the meatloaf from the Ninja Foodi and allow to cool.

8. Serve with sauce and enjoy.

**Nutritional Information Per Serving:**

Calories 574; carbohydrates: 23.2g; protein: 46.6g; fat: 32.7g

# Tangy Pork Carnitas

(Prepping time: 10 minutes| Cooking Time: 25 minutes |Serves: 6)

**Ingredients:**

- 2 pounds pork shoulder, bone-in
- 2 tablespoons butter, melted
- 2 oranges, juiced
- Ground black pepper and salt to taste
- 1 teaspoon garlic powder
- 5-6 warmed carnitas

**Preparation:**

1. Season the pork with salt, garlic powder, and black pepper.

2. Take Ninja Foodi multi-cooker, arrange it over a cooking platform, and open the top lid.

3. In the pot, add the butter; Select "sear/sauté" mode and select "md: hi" pressure level.

4. Press "stop/start." After about 4-5 minutes, the butter will start simmering.

5. Add the meat and stir cook for about 2-3 minutes to brown evenly. Stir in orange juice.

6. Seal the multi-cooker by locking it with the pressure lid; ensure to keep the pressure release valve locked/sealed.

7. Select "pressure" mode and select the "HI" pressure level. Then, set timer to 15 minutes and press "stop/start"; it will start the cooking process by building up inside pressure.

8. When the timer goes off, naturally release inside pressure for about 8-10 minutes. Then, quick-release pressure by adjusting the pressure valve to the vent.

9. Select "broil" mode and select the "HI" pressure level. Then, set timer to 15 minutes and press "stop/start"; it will start the cooking process by building up inside pressure.

10. When the timer goes off, quick release pressure by adjusting the pressure valve to the vent.

11. After pressure gets released, open the pressure lid.

12. Shred the meat and remove the bones. Add the mixture over the carnitas; fold and serve warm.

**Nutritional Information Per Serving:**

Calories: 486, Fat: 32g, Carbs: 9g, Protein: 34g

# Beef Stew Recipe from Ethiopia

(Prepping time: 6 minutes| Cooking Time: 55 minutes |Serves: 2)

## Ingredients:

- 1-pound beef stew meat, cut into chunks
- ¼ teaspoon turmeric powder
- 1 tablespoon garam masala
- 1 tablespoon coriander powder
- 1 teaspoon cumin
- ¼ teaspoon ground nutmeg
- 2 teaspoons smoked paprika
- ¼ teaspoon black pepper
- 2 tablespoons ghee
- 1 onion, chopped
- 1 tablespoon ginger, grated
- 2 cloves of garlic, grated
- 1 tablespoon onions
- 3 tablespoons tomato paste
- ½ teaspoon sugar
- Salt and pepper to taste
- 1 cup water

## Preparation:

1.  In a mixing bowl, combine the first 8 ingredients and allow to marinate in the fridge for at least 4 hours.

2.  Press the sauté button and heat the oil. Sauté the onion, ginger, and garlic until fragrant. Stir in the marinated beef and allow to sear button for 3 minutes.

3.  Stir in the rest of the ingredients.

4.  Install pressure lid. Close Ninja Foodi, press the pressure button, choose high settings, and set time to 50 minutes.

5.  Once done cooking, do a quick release.

6.  Serve and enjoy.

## Nutritional Information Per Serving:

Calories 591; carbohydrates: 11.5g; protein: 83.5g; fat: 23.4g

# Potatoes, Beefy-Cheesy Way

(Prepping time: 5 minutes| Cooking Time: 25 minutes |Serves: 2)

**Ingredients:**

- ½ pounds ground beef
- 2 large potatoes, peeled and chopped
- ¾ cup cheddar cheese, shredded
- ¼ cup chicken broth
- ½ tablespoon Italian seasoning mix
- Salt and pepper to taste

**Preparation:**

1. Press the sauté button on the Ninja Foodi and stir in the beef. Sear button the meat until some of the oil has rendered.
2. Add the rest of the ingredients.
3. Install pressure lid.
4. Close Ninja Foodi, press the pressure button, choose high settings, and set time to 20 minutes.
5. Once done cooking, do a quick release.

**Nutritional Information Per Serving:**

Calories 801; carbohydrates: 66.8g; protein: 53.4g; fat: 35.6g

# Orecchiette and Pork Ragu

(Prepping time: 10 minutes| Cooking Time: 25 minutes |Serves: 6)

**Ingredients:**

- 3 tablespoons extra-virgin olive oil, divided
- 1-pound pork shoulder, cut into large pieces
- 1 small onion, diced
- 1 carrot, diced
- 1 celery stalk, diced
- 1 garlic clove, minced
- 1 can crushed tomatoes
- 1 can tomato purée
- 1 cup red wine
- 2 cups beef stock
- 1 box orecchiette pasta
- 1 teaspoon sea salt
- 1 teaspoon Italian seasoning
- 1 bunch Tuscan kale, ribs and stems removed, torn

- ¼ cup unsalted butter, cubed
- ½ cup grated Parmesan cheese

**Preparation:**

1. Select sear/sauté and set to HI. Select start/stop to begin. Let preheat for 5 minutes.

2. Place 2 tablespoons of oil in the pot. Once hot, add the pork pieces and sear on all sides, turning until brown, about 10 minutes in total. Transfer the pork to a large plate and set aside.

3. Add onion, carrot, and celery and cook for about 5 minutes. Add the garlic and cook for 1 minute.

4. Add the crushed tomatoes, tomato purée, red wine, beef stock, pasta, salt, and Italian seasoning. Place the pork back in the pot. Assemble pressure lid, making sure the pressure release valve is in the SEAL position.

5. Select pressure and set to LO. Set time to 0 minutes. Select start/stop to begin.

6. When pressure cooking is complete, allow pressure to naturally release for 10 minutes. After 10 minutes, quick release remaining pressure by moving the pressure release valve to the vent position. Carefully remove lid when unit has finished releasing pressure.

7. Pull the pork pieces apart using two forks. Add the remaining 1 tablespoon of olive oil, kale, butter, and Parmesan cheese and stir until the butter melts and the kale is wilted. Serve.

**Nutritional Information Per Serving:**

Calories: 556, Fat: 21g, Carbs: 59g, Protein: 30g

# Authentic Beginner Friendly Pork Belly

(Prepping time: 10 minutes| Cooking Time: 10 minutes |Serves: 4)

**Ingredients:**

- 1-pound pork belly
- ½-1 cup white wine vinegar
- 1 garlic clove
- 1 tablespoon olive oil
- Salt and pepper to taste

**Preparation:**

1. Set your Ninja Foodi to "sauté" mode and add oil, let it heat up

2. Add pork and sear for 2-3 minutes until both sides are golden and crispy

3. Add vinegar until about a quarter inch, season with salt, pepper and garlic

4. Add garlic clove and Saute until the liquid comes to a boil

5. Lock lid and cook on high pressure for 40 minutes

6. Once done, quick release pressure

7. Slice the meat and serve with the sauce

8. Enjoy!

**Nutritional Information Per Serving:**

Calories: 331, Fat: 21g, Carbs: 2g, Protein: 19g

# Deliciously Spicy Pork Salad Bowl

(Prepping time: 10 minutes| Cooking Time: 90 minutes |Serves: 6)

**Ingredients:**

- 4 pounds pork shoulder
- Butter as needed
- 2 teaspoons salt
- 2 cups chicken stock
- 1 teaspoon smoked paprika powder
- 1 teaspoon garlic powder
- 1 teaspoon black pepper
- 1 pinch dried oregano leaves
- 4 tablespoons coconut oil
- 6 garlic cloves

**Preparation:**

1. Remove rind from pork and cut meat from bone, slice into large chunks
2. Trim fat off met
3. Set your Foodi to Saute mode and add oil, let it heat up
4. Once the oil is hot, layer chunks of meat in the bottom of the pot and Saute for around 30 minutes until browned
5. While the meat is being browned, peel garlic cloves and cut into small chunks
6. Once the meat is browned, transfer it to a large sized bowl
7. Add a few tablespoons of chicken stock to the pot an deglaze it, scraping off browned bits
8. Transfer browned bits to the bowl with meat chunks
9. Repeat if any more meat is left
10. Once done, add garlic, oregano leaves, smoked paprika, Garlic powder, pepper and salt to the meat owl and mix it up
11. Add all chicken stock to pot and bring to a simmer over Saute mode
12. Once done, return seasoned meat to the pot and lock lid, cook on high pressure for 45 minutes. Release pressure naturally over 10 minutes
13. Open lid and shred the meat using fork, transfer shredded meat to a bowl and pour cooking liquid through a mesh to separate fat into the bowl with shredded meat
14. Serve with lime and enjoy!

**Nutritional Information Per Serving:**

Calories: 307, Fat: 23g, Carbs: 8g, Protein: 15g

# Special "Swiss" Pork chops

(Prepping time: 5 minutes| Cooking Time: 18 minutes |Serves: 4)

**Ingredients:**

- ½ cup Swiss cheese, shredded
- 4 pork chops, bone-in
- 6 bacon strips, cut in half
- Salt and pepper to taste
- 1 tablespoon butter

**Preparation:**

1. Season pork chops with salt and pepper
2. Set your Foodi to sauté mode and add butter, let the butter heat up
3. Add pork chops and sauté for 3 minutes on each side
4. Add bacon strips and Swiss cheese
5. Lock lid and cook on Medium-low pressure for 15 minutes
6. Release pressure naturally over 10 minutes
7. Transfer steaks to serving platter, serve and enjoy!

**Nutritional Information Per Serving:**

Calories: 483, Fat: 40g, Carbohydrates:0.7g, Protein: 27g


# Healthy Cranberry BBQ Pork

(Prepping time: 10 minutes| Cooking Time: 45 minutes |Serves: 4)

**Ingredients:**

- 3-4 pounds pork shoulder, boneless, fat trimmed
- 3 tablespoons liquid smoke
- 2 tablespoons tomato paste
- 2 cups fresh cranberries
- ¼ cup hot sauce
- 1/3 cup blackstrap molasses
- ½ cup water
- ½ cup apple cider vinegar
- 1 teaspoon salt
- 1 tablespoons adobo sauce
- 1 cup tomato puree
- 1 chipotle pepper in adobo sauce, diced

**Preparation:**

1. Cut pork against halves/thirds and keep it on the side

2. Set your Ninja Foodi to "sauté" mode and let it heat up

3. Add cranberries and water to the pot

4. Let them simmer for 4-5 minutes until cranberries start to pop, add rest of the sauce ingredients and simmer for 5 minutes more

5. Add pork to the pot and lock lid

6. Cook on high pressure for 40 minutes

7. Quick release pressure

8. Use fork to shred the pork and serve on your favorite greens

**Nutritional Information Per Serving:**

Calories: 250, Fat: 17g, Carbs: 5g, Protein: 15g

# St. Patty's Corned Beef Recipe

(Prepping time: 6 minutes| Cooking Time: 60 minutes |Serves: 2)

**Ingredients:**

- 2 cloves of garlic, chopped

- ½ onion, quartered

- 1 ¼ pounds corned beef brisket, cut in large slices

- 3-oz. Beer

- 1 cup water

- 2 small carrots, roughly chopped

- 1 small potato, chopped

- ½ head cabbage, cut into four pieces

**Preparation:**

1. In the Ninja Foodi, place the garlic, onion, corned beef brisket, beer, and water. Season with salt and pepper to taste.

2. Install pressure lid. Close Ninja Foodi, press the pressure button, choose high settings, and set time to 50 minutes.

3. Once done cooking, do a quick release. Open the lid and take out the meat. Shred the meat using fork and place it back into the Ninja Foodi.

4. Stir in the vegetables.

5. Install pressure lid. Close the lid and seal the vent and press the pressure button. Cook for another 10 minutes. Do quick release.

**Nutritional Information Per Serving:**

Calories 758; carbohydrates: 45.8g; protein: 43.1g; fat: 44.7g

# Chapter 3: Chicken and Poultry Recipes

## Fully-Stuffed Whole Chicken

(Prepping time: 10 minutes| Cooking Time: 8 hours |Serves: 6)

**Ingredients:**

- 1 cup mozzarella cheese
- 4 whole garlic cloves, peeled
- 1 whole chicken (2 pounds), cleaned and pat dried
- Salt and pepper as needed
- 2 tablespoons fresh lemon juice

**Preparation:**

1. Stuff the chicken cavity with garlic cloves and mozzarella cheese
2. Season chicken generously with salt and pepper
3. Transfer chicken to your Ninja Foodi and drizzle lemon juice
4. Lock lid and set to "Slow Cooker" mode, let it cook on LOW for 8 hours
5. Once doe, serve and enjoy!

**Nutritional Information Per Serving:**

Calories: 309, Fat: 12g, Carbohydrates: 1.6g, Protein: 45g

## A Genuine Hassel Back Chicken

(Prepping time: 5 minutes| Cooking Time: 60 minutes |Serves: 4)

**Ingredients:**

- 4 tablespoons butter
- Salt and pepper to taste
- 2 cups fresh mozzarella cheese, thinly sliced
- 8 large chicken breasts
- 4 large Roma tomatoes, thinly sliced

**Preparation:**

1. Make few deep slits in chicken breasts, season with salt and pepper
2. Stuff mozzarella cheese slices and tomatoes in chicken slits
3. Grease Ninja Foodi pot with butter and arrange stuffed chicken breasts
4. Lock lid and BAKE/ROAST for 1 hour at 365 degrees F
5. Serve and enjoy!

**Nutritional Information Per Serving:**

Calories: 278, Fat: 15g, Carbohydrates: 3.8g, Protein: 15g

# Elegant Chicken Stock

(Prepping time: 10 minutes| Cooking Time: 2hours |Serves: 4)

**Ingredients:**

- 2 pounds meaty chicken bones
- ¼ teaspoon salt
- 3 and ½ cups water

**Preparation:**

1. Place chicken parts in Foodi and season with salt

2. Add water, place the pressure cooker lid and seal the valve, cook on HIGH pressure for 90 minutes

3. Release the pressure naturally over 10 minutes

4. Line a colander with cheesecloth and place it over a large bowl, pour chicken parts and stock into the colander and strain out the chicken and bones

5. Let the stock cool and let it peel off any layer of fat that might accumulate on the surface

6. Use as needed!

**Nutritional Information Per Serving:**

Calories: 51, Fat: 3g, Carbohydrates: 1g, Protein: 6g

# Sensational Lime and Chicken Chili

(Prepping time: 10 minutes| Cooking Time: 23 minutes |Serves: 6)

**Ingredients:**

- ¼ cup cooking wine (Keto-Friendly)
- ½ cup organic chicken broth
- 1 onion, diced
- 1 teaspoon salt
- ½ teaspoon paprika
- 5 garlic cloves, minced
- 1 tablespoon lime juice
- ¼ cup butter
- 2 pounds chicken thighs
- 1 teaspoon dried parsley
- 3 green chilies, chopped

**Preparation:**

1. Set your Ninja-Foodi to Sauté mode and add onion and garlic

2. Sauté for 3 minutes, add remaining ingredients

3. Lock lid and cook on Medium-HIGH pressure for 20 minutes

4. Release pressure naturally over 10 minutes

5. Serve and enjoy!

**Nutritional Information Per Serving:**

Calories: 282, Fat: 15g, Carbohydrates: 6g, Protein: 27g

# Shredded Up Salsa Chicken

(Prepping time: 5 minutes| Cooking Time: 20 minutes |Serves: 4)

**Ingredients:**

- 1 pound chicken breast, skin and bones removed
- ¾ teaspoon cumin
- ½ teaspoon salt
- Pinch of oregano
- Pepper to taste
- 1 cup chunky salsa Keto friendly

**Preparation:**

1. Season chicken with spices and add to Ninja Foodi
2. Cover with salsa and lock lid, cook on HIGH pressure for 20 minutes
3. Quick release pressure
4. Add chicken to a platter and shred the chicken
5. Serve and enjoy!

**Nutritional Information Per Serving:**

Calories: 125, Fat: 3g, Carbohydrates: 2g, Protein: 22g

# Mexico's Favorite Chicken Soup

(Prepping time: 5 minutes| Cooking Time: 20 minutes |Serves: 4)

**Ingredients:**

- 2 cups chicken, shredded
- 4 tablespoons olive oil
- ½ cup cilantro, chopped
- 8 cups chicken broth
- 1/3 cup salsa
- 1 teaspoon onion powder
- ½ cup scallions, chopped
- 4 ounces green chilies, chopped
- ½ teaspoon habanero, minced
- 1 cup celery root, chopped

- 1 teaspoon cumin
- 1 teaspoon garlic powder
- Salt and pepper to taste

**Preparation:**

1. Add all ingredients to Ninja Foodi
2. Stir and lock lid, cook on HIGH pressure for 10 minutes
3. Release pressure naturally over 10 minutes
4. Serve and enjoy!

**Nutritional Information Per Serving:**

Calories: 204, Fat: 14g, Carbohydrates: 4g, Protein: 14g

# Perfectly Braised Chicken Thigh with Chokeful Of Mushrooms

(Prepping time: 10 minutes| Cooking Time: 30 minutes |Serves: 4)

**Ingredients:**

- 4 chicken thigh, bone in- skin on
- 1 teaspoon salt
- 1 tablespoon olive oil
- ½ small onion, sliced
- ½ cup white wine vinegar
- ½ cup chicken stock
- 1 cup frozen artichoke hearts, thawed and drained
- 1 bay leaf
- Fresh ground black pepper
- ¼ cup heavy cream

**Preparation:**

1. Set your Foodi to Sauté mode and set it to Medium-HIGH, pre-heat for 5 minutes
2. Pour olive oil and wait until it shimmers
3. Add chicken thighs, skin side-side down, cook for 4-5 minutes
4. Turn and sear the other side for 1 minute
5. Remove from pot
6. Add onion, sprinkle with remaining salt, cook for 2 minutes more until tender
7. Add wine and bring to a boil. Cook for 2-3 minutes, until reduced by half
8. Add chicken stock, artichoke hearts, bay leaf, thyme, several grinds of pepper, stir well
9. Place chicken thigh back to the pot (skin side up), lock pressure lid into place and seal the valve
10. Select pressure mode to HIGH and cook for 5 minutes
11. Once done, quick release pressure

12. use tongs to transfer chicken to Reversible Rack in the upper position, add mushrooms to sauce and stir. Set rack in the pot

13. Close with crisping lid and select Bake/Roast, adjust the temperature to 375 degrees F, cook for 12 minutes

14. Once done, open lid and transfer chicken to the platter, add heavy cream and stir into the sauce. stir in sauce, season with salt and pepper

15. Pour sauce and vegetables around chicken, serve and enjoy!

**Nutritional Information Per Serving:**

Calories: 268, Fat: 20g, Carbohydrates: 7g, Protein: 19g

# Cabbage and Chicken Meatballs

(Prepping time: 10 minutes + 30 minutes| Cooking Time: 4-6 minutes |Serves: 4)

**Ingredients:**

- 1 pound ground chicken
- ¼ cup heavy whip cream
- 2 teaspoons salt
- ½ teaspoon ground caraway seeds
- 1 and ½ teaspoons fresh ground black pepper, divided
- 1/4 teaspoon ground allspice
- 4-6 cups green cabbage, thickly chopped
- ½ cup almond milk
- 2 tablespoons unsalted butter

**Preparation:**

1. Transfer meat to a bowl and add cream, 1 teaspoon salt, caraway, ½ teaspoon pepper, allspice and mix it well

2. Let the mixture chill for 30 minutes

3. Once the mixture is ready, use your hands to scoop the mixture into meatballs

4. Add half of your balls to Ninja Foodi pot and cover with half of the cabbage

5. Add remaining balls and cover with rest of the cabbage

6. Add milk, pats of butter, season with salt and pepper

7. Lock lid and cook on HIGH pressure for 4 minutes

8. Quick release pressure

9. Unlock lid and serve

10. Enjoy!

**Nutritional Information Per Serving:**

Calories: 294, Fat: 26g, Carbohydrates: 4g, Protein: 12g

# Taiwanese Chicken Delight

(Prepping time: 5 minutes| Cooking Time: 10 minutes |Serves: 4)

## Ingredients:

- 6 dried red chilis
- ¼ cup sesame oil
- 2 tablespoons ginger
- ¼ cup garlic, minced
- ¼ cup red wine vinegar
- ¼ cup coconut aminos
- Salt as needed
- 1.2 teaspoon xanthan gum (for the finish)
- ¼ cup Thai basil, chopped

## Preparation:

1. Set your Ninja Foodi to Saute mode and add ginger, chilis, garlic and Saute for 2 minutes
2. Add remaining ingredients
3. Lock lid and cook on HIGH pressure for 10 minutes
4. Quick release pressure
5. Serve and enjoy!

## Nutritional Information Per Serving:

Calories: 307, Fat: 15g, Carbohydrates: 7g, Protein: 31g

# Lemon and Chicken Extravaganza

(Prepping time: 5 minutes| Cooking Time: 18 minutes |Serves: 4)

## Ingredients:

- 4 bone-in, skin on chicken thighs
- Salt and pepper to taste
- 2 tablespoons butter, divided
- 2 teaspoons garlic, minced
- ½ cup herbed chicken stock
- ½ cup heavy whip cream
- ½ a lemon, juiced

## Preparation:

1. Season your chicken thighs generously with salt and pepper
2. Set your Foodi to sauté mode and add oil, let it heat up
3. Add thigh, Sauté both sides for 6 minutes

4.  Remove thigh to a platter and keep it on the side

5.  Add garlic, cook for 2 minutes

6.  Whisk in chicken stock, heavy cream, lemon juice and gently stir

7.  Bring the mix to a simmer and reintroduce chicken

8.  Lock lid and cook for 10 minutes on HIGH pressure

9.  Release pressure over 10 minutes

10. Serve and enjoy!

**Nutritional Information Per Serving:**

Calories: 294, Fat: 26g, Carbohydrates: 4g, Protein: 12g

# Lemon and Butter Chicken Extravagant

(Prepping time: 10 minutes| Cooking Time: 10 minutes |Serves: 4)

**Ingredients:**

*   4 bone-in, skin on chicken thighs

*   salt and pepper as needed

*   2 tablespoons butter, divided

*   2 teaspoons garlic, minced

*   1/2 cup herbed chicken stock

*   1/2 cup heavy whip cream

*   1/2 a lemon, juiced

**Preparation:**

1.  Season chicken thighs with salt and pepper

2.  Set your Ninja Foodi to Sauté mode and add oil, let it heat up

3.  Add chicken thighs and saute both sides until golden, total for 6 minutes

4.  Remove thighs to a plater and keep it on the side

5.  Add garlic and cook for 2 minutes

6.  Whisk in chicken stock, heavy cream, lemon juice and stir, bring the sauce to simmer and reintroduce the chicken

7.  Lock lid and cook for 10 minutes on HIGH pressure

8.  Release pressure naturally over 10 minutes

9.  Serve warm and enjoy!

**Nutritional Information Per Serving:**

Calories: 294, Fat: 26g, Carbohydrates: 4g, Protein: 12g

# Juicy Sesame Garlic Chicken Wings

(Prepping time: 10 minutes| Cooking Time: 25 minutes |Serves: 4)

**Ingredients:**

- 24 chicken wing segments
- 2 tablespoons toasted sesame oil
- 2 tablespoons Asian-Chile-Garlic sauce
- 2 tablespoons stevia
- 2 garlic cloves, minced
- 1 tablespoon toasted sesame seeds

**Preparation:**

1. Add 1 cup water to Foodi's inner pot, place reversible rack in the pot in lower portions, place chicken wings in the rack
2. Place lid into place and seal the valve
3. Select pressure mode to HIGH and cook for 10 minutes
4. Make the glaze by taking a large bowl and whisking in sesame oil, Chile-Garlic sauce, honey and garlic
5. Once the chicken is cooked, quick release the pressure and remove pressure lid
6. Remove rack from the pot and empty remaining water
7. Return inner pot to the base
8. Cover with crisping lid and select Air Crisp mode, adjust the temperature to 375 degrees F, pre-heat for 3 minutes
9. While the Foodi pre-heats, add wings to the sauce and toss well to coat it
10. Transfer wings to the basket, leaving any excess sauce in the bowl
11. Place the basket in Foodi and close with Crisping mode, select Air Crisp mode and let it cook for 8 minutes, gently toss the wings and let it cook for 8 minutes more
12. Once done, drizzle any sauce and sprinkle sesame seeds
13. Enjoy!

**Nutritional Information Per Serving:**

Calories: 440, Fat: 32g, Carbohydrates: 12g, Protein: 28g

# Spicy Hot Paprika Chicken

(Prepping time: 10 minutes| Cooking Time: 5 minutes |Serves: 4)

**Ingredients:**

- 4 pieces (4 ounces each) chicken breast, skin on
- Salt and pepper as needed
- 1 tablespoon olive oil

- ½ cup sweet onion, chopped
- ½ cup heavy whip cream
- 2 teaspoons smoked paprika
- ½ cup sour cream
- 2 tablespoons fresh parsley, chopped

**Preparation:**

1. Lightly season the chicken with salt and pepper
2. Set your Ninja Foodi to Sauté mode and add oil, let the oil heat up
3. Add chicken and sear both sides until properly browned, should take about 15 minutes
4. Remove chicken and transfer them to a plate
5. Take a skillet and place it over medium heat, add onion and Saute for 4 minutes until tender
6. Stir in cream, paprika and bring the liquid simmer
7. Return chicken to the skillet and alongside any juices
8. Transfer the whole mixture to your Ninja Foodi and lock lid, cook on HIGH pressure for 5 minutes
9. Release pressure naturally over 10 minutes
10. Stir in sour cream, serve and enjoy!

**Nutritional Information Per Serving:**

Calories: 389, Fat: 30g, Carbohydrates: 4g, Protein: 25g

# Creative Cabbage and Chicken Meatball

(Prepping time: 15 minutes| Cooking Time: 4 minutes |Serves: 4)

**Ingredients:**

- 1 pound ground chicken
- 1/4 cup heavy whip cream
- 2 teaspoon salt
- 1/2 teaspoon ground caraway seeds
- 1 and 1/2 teaspoons fresh ground black pepper, divided
- 1/4 teaspoon ground allspice
- 4-6 cups green cabbage, thickly chopped
- 1/2 cup almond milk
- 2 tablespoons unsalted butter

**Preparation:**

1. Transfer meat to a bowl
2. Add cream, 1 teaspoon salt, caraway, 1/2 teaspoon pepper, allspice and mix well
3. Refrigerate the mixture for 30 minutes
4. Once the mixture is cool, use your hands to scoop the mixture into meatballs

5. Place half of the balls to your Ninja Foodi pot and cover with half of cabbage
6. Add remaining balls and cover with remaining cabbage
7. Add milk, pats of butter and sprinkle 1 teaspoon salt, 1 teaspoon pepper
8. Lock lid and cook on HIGH pressure for 4 minutes
9. Quick release pressure
10. Unlock lid and serve
11. Enjoy!

**Nutritional Information Per Serving:**

Calories: 338, Fat: 23g, Carbohydrates: 7g, Protein: 23g

# Hot Turkey Cutlets

(Prepping time: 10 minutes| Cooking Time: 15 minutes |Serves: 4)

**Ingredients:**

- 1 teaspoon Greek seasoning
- 1 pound turkey cutlets
- 2 tablespoons olive oil
- 1 teaspoon turmeric powder
- ½ cup almond flour

**Preparation:**

1. Take a bowl and add Greek seasoning, turmeric powder, almond flour and mix well
2. Dredge turkey cutlets in the bowl and let it sit for 30 minutes
3. Set your Ninja Foodi to Sauté mode and add oil, let it heat up
4. Add cutlets and Sauté for 2 minutes
5. Lock lid and cook on Low-Medium Pressure for 20 minutes
6. Release pressure naturally over 10 minutes
7. Take the dish out, serve and enjoy!

**Nutritional Information Per Serving:**

Calories: 340, Fat: 19g, Carbohydrates: 3.7g, Protein: 36g

# Pulled Up Keto Friendly Chicken Tortilla's

(Prepping time: 15 minutes| Cooking Time: 15 minutes |Serves: 4)

**Ingredients:**

- 1 tablespoon avocado oil
- 1 pound pastured organic boneless chicken breasts
- ½ cup orange juice
- 2 teaspoons gluten-free Worcestershire sauce

- 1 teaspoon garlic powder
- 1 teaspoon salt
- ½ teaspoon chili powder
- ½ teaspoon paprika

**Preparation:**

1. Set your Ninja Foodi to Sauté mode and add oil, let the oil heat up
2. Add chicken on top, take a bowl and add remaining ingredients mix well
3. Pour the mixture over chicken
4. Lock lid and cook on HIGH pressure for 15 minutes
5. Release pressure naturally over 10 minutes
6. Shred the chicken and serve over salad green shell such as cabbage or lettuce
7. Enjoy!

**Nutritional Information Per Serving:**

Calories: 338, Fat: 23g, Carbohydrates: 10g, Protein: 23g


# Ham-Stuffed Generous Turkey Rolls

(Prepping time: 10 minutes| Cooking Time: 20 minutes |For 8 servings)

**Ingredients:**

- 4 tablespoons fresh sage leaves
- 8 ham slices
- 8 (6 ounces each) turkey cutlets
- Salt and pepper to taste
- 2 tablespoons butter, melted

**Preparation:**

1. Season turkey cutlets with salt and pepper
2. Roll turkey cutlets and wrap each of them with ham slices tightly
3. Coat each roll with butter and gently place sage leaves evenly over each cutlet
4. Transfer them to your Ninja Foodi
5. Lock lid and select the "Bake/Roast" mode, bake for 10 minutes a 360 degrees F
6. Open the lid and gently give it a flip, lock lid again and bake for 10 minutes more
7. Once done, serve and enjoy!

**Nutritional Information Per Serving:**

Calories: 467, Fat: 24g, Carbohydrates: 1.7g, Protein: 56g

# The Great Hainanese Chicken

(Prepping time: 20 minutes | Cooking Time: 4 hours |Serves: 4)

**Ingredients:**

- 1 ounces ginger, peeled
- 6 garlic cloves, crushed
- 6 bundles cilantro/basil leaves
- 1 teaspoon salt
- 1 tablespoon sesame oil
- 3 (1 and ½ pounds each) chicken meat, ready to cook

**For Dip**

- 2 tablespoons ginger, minced
- 1 teaspoon garlic, minced
- 1 tablespoon chicken stock
- 1 teaspoon sesame oil
- ½ teaspoon sugar
- Salt to taste

**Preparation:**

1. Add chicken, garlic, ginger, leaves, and salt in your Ninja Food
2. Add enough water to fully submerge chicken, lock lid cook on SLOW COOK mode on LOW for 4 hours
3. Release pressure naturally
4. Take chicken out of pot and chill for 10 minutes
5. Take a bowl and add all the dipping ingredients and blend well in a food processor
6. Take chicken out of ice bath and drain, chop into serving pieces
7. Arrange onto a serving platter
8. Brush chicken with sesame oil
9. Serve with ginger dip
10. Enjoy!

**Nutritional Information Per Serving:**

Calories: 535, Fat: 45g, Carbohydrates: 5g, Protein: 28g

# Funky-Garlic and turkey Breasts

(Prepping time: 10 minutes| Cooking Time: 17 minutes |Serves: 4)

## Ingredients:

- ½ teaspoon garlic powder
- 4 tablespoons butter
- ¼ teaspoon dried oregano
- 1 pound turkey breasts, boneless
- 1 teaspoon pepper
- ½ teaspoon salt
- ¼ teaspoon dried basil

## Preparation:

1. Season turkey on both sides generously with garlic, dried oregano, dried basil, salt and pepper
2. Set your Ninja Foodi to sauté mode and add butter, let the butter melt
3. Add turkey breasts and sauté for 2 minutes on each side
4. Lock the lid and select the "Bake/Roast" setting, bake for 15 minutes at 355 degrees F
5. Serve and enjoy once done!

## Nutritional Information Per Serving:

Calories: 223, Fat: 13g, Carbohydrates: 5g, Protein: 19g

# Bruschetta Chicken Meal

(Prepping time: 5 minutes| Cooking Time: 9 minutes |Serves: 4)

**Ingredients:**

- 2 tablespoons balsamic vinegar
- 1/3 cup olive oil
- 2 teaspoons garlic cloves, minced
- 1 teaspoon black pepper
- ½ teaspoon salt
- ½ cup sun-dried tomatoes, in olive oil
- 2 pounds chicken breasts, quartered, boneless
- 2 tablespoons fresh basil, chopped

**Preparation:**

1. Take a bowl and whisk in vinegar, oil, garlic, pepper, salt
2. Fold in tomatoes, basil and add breast, mix well
3. Transfer to fridge and let it sit for 30 minutes
4. Add everything to Ninja Foodi and lock lid, cook on High Pressure for 9 minutes
5. Quick release pressure
6. Serve and enjoy!

**Nutritional Information Per Serving:**

Calories: 480, Fat: 26g, Carbohydrates: 4g, Protein: 52g

# Chapter 4: Seafood and Fish Recipes

## Salmon in Dill Sauce

(Prepping time: 10 minutes| Cooking Time: 2 hours |Serves: 6)

**Ingredients**:

- 2 cups water
- 1 cup chicken broth
- 2 tablespoons fresh lemon juice
- ¼ cup fresh dill, chopped
- ½ teaspoon lemon zest, grated
- 6 (4-ounce) salmon fillets
- Salt and ground black pepper, as required

**Preparation:**

1. In the pot of Ninja Foodi, mix together the water, broth, lemon juice, lemon juice, dill and lemon zest.
2. Arrange the salmon fillets on top, skin side down and sprinkle with salt and black pepper.
3. Close the Ninja Foodi with crisping lid and select "Slow Cooker".
4. Set on "Low" for 1-2 hours.
5. Press "Start/Stop" to begin cooking.
6. Open the lid and serve hot.

**Nutritional Information Per Serving:**

Calories: 164, Fat: 7.4 g, Saturated Fat: 1.1 g, Trans Fat: 6.3 g, Carbohydrates: 1.6 g, Fiber 0.4 g, Sodium 210 mg, Protein: 23.3 g

## Buttered Salmon

(Prepping time: 10 minutes| Cooking Time: 10 minutes |Serves: 2)

**Ingredients**:

- 2 (6-ounce) salmon fillets
- Salt and ground black pepper, as required
- 1 tablespoon butter, melted

**Preparation:**

1. Arrange the greased "Cook & Crisp Basket" in the pot of Ninja Foodi.
2. Close the Ninja Foodi with crisping lid and select "Air Crisp".
3. Set the temperature to 360 degrees F for 5 minutes.
4. Press "Start/Stop" to begin preheating.

5. Season each salmon fillet with salt and black pepper and then coat with the melted butter.

6. After preheating, open the lid.

7. Arrange the salmon fillets into the prepared "Cook & Crisp Basket" in a single layer.

8. Close the Ninja Foodi with crisping lid and select "Air Crisp".

9. Set the temperature to 360 degrees F for 10 minutes.

10. Press "Start/Stop" to begin cooking.

11. Open the lid and serve hot.

**Nutritional Information Per Serving:**

Calories: 276, Fat: 16.3 g, Saturated Fat: 5.2 g, Trans Fat: 11.1 g, Carbohydrates: 0 g, Fiber 0 g, Sodium 193 mg, Protein: 33.1 g

# Spicy Salmon Paprika

(Prepping time: 10 minutes| Cooking Time: 7 minutes |Serves: 4)

**Ingredients:**

- 2 wild-caught salmon fillets, 1 to 1 and ½ inches thick
- 2 teaspoons avocado oil
- 2 teaspoons paprika
- Salt and pepper to taste
- Green herbs to garnish

**Preparation:**

1. Season salmon fillets with salt, pepper, paprika, and olive oil

2. Place Crisping basket in your Ninja Foodi, and pre-heat your Ninja Foodie at 390 degrees F

3. Place insert insider your Foodi and place the fillet in the insert, lock Air Crisping lid and cook for 7 minutes

4. Once done, serve the fish with herbs on top

5. Enjoy!

**Nutritional Information Per Serving:**

Calories: 246, Fat: 11g, Saturated Fat: 4 g, Carbohydrates: 1.8 g, Fiber: 2 g, Sodium: mg, Protein: 35 g

# Buttery Scallops

(Prepping time: 10 minutes| Cooking Time: 5 minutes |Serves: 4)

**Ingredients:**

- 4 garlic cloves, minced
- 4 tablespoons rosemary, chopped
- 2 pounds sea scallops

- 12 cup butter
- Salt and pepper to taste

**Preparation:**

1. Set your Ninja Foodi to Saute mode and add butter, rosemary, and garlic
2. Saute for 1 minute
3. Add scallops, salt, and pepper
4. Saute for 2 minutes
5. Lock Crisping lid and Crisp for 3 minutes at 350 degrees F
6. Serve and enjoy!

**Nutritional Information Per Serving:**

Calories: 279, Fat: 16g, Saturated Fat: 4 g, Carbohydrates: 5 g, Fiber: 2 g, Sodium: 964 mg, Protein: 25 g

# Hearty Cod Fillets

(Prepping time: 10 minutes| Cooking Time: 5-10 minutes |Serves: 4)

**Ingredients:**

- 1 pound frozen codfish fillets
- 2 garlic cloves, halved
- 1 cup chicken broth
- ½ cup packed parsley
- 2 tablespoons oregano
- 2 tablespoons almonds, sliced½ teaspoon paprika

**Preparation:**

1. Take the fish out of the freezer and let it defrost
2. Take a food processor and stir in garlic, oregano, parsley, paprika, 1 tablespoon almond and process
3. Set your Ninja Foodi to "SAUTE" mode and add olive oil, let it heat up
4. Add remaining almonds and toast, transfer to a towel
5. Pour broth in a pot and add the herb mixture
6. Cut fish into 4 pieces and place in a steamer basket, transfer steamer basket to the pot
7. Lock lid and cook on HIGH Pressure for 3 minutes
8. Quick-release Pressure once has done
9. Serve steamed fish by pouring over the sauce
10. Enjoy!

**Nutritional Information Per Serving:**

Calories: 246, Fat: 10g, Saturated Fat: 3 g, Carbohydrates: 8 g, Fiber: 2 g, Sodium: mg, Protein: 15 g

# Spicy Catfish

(Prepping time: 10 minutes| Cooking Time: 13 minutes |Serves: 2)

**Ingredients**:

- 2 tablespoons almond flour
- 1 teaspoon red chili powder
- ½ teaspoon paprika
- ½ teaspoon garlic powder
- Salt, as required
- 2 (6-ounces) catfish fillets
- 1 tablespoon olive oil

**Preparation:**

1. Arrange the greased "Cook & Crisp Basket" in the pot of Ninja Foodi.
2. Close the Ninja Foodi with crisping lid and select "Air Crisp".
3. Set the temperature to 400 degrees F for 5 minutes.
4. Press "Start/Stop" to begin preheating.
5. In a bowl, mix together the flour, paprika, garlic powder and salt.
6. Add the catfish fillets and coat with the mixture evenly.
7. Now, coat each fillet with oil.
8. After preheating, open the lid.
9. Place the catfish fillets into the "Cook & Crisp Basket".
10. Close the Ninja Foodi with crisping lid and select "Air Crisp".
11. Set the temperature to 400 degrees F for 13 minutes.
12. Press "Start/Stop" to begin cooking.
13. Flip the fish fillets once halfway through.
14. Open the lid and serve hot.

**Nutritional Information Per Serving:**

Calories: 458, Fat: 34.2 g, Saturated Fat: 4.4 g, Trans Fat: 29.8 g, Carbohydrates: 7.5 g, Fiber 3.7 g, Sodium 191 mg, Protein: 32.8 g

# Parmesan Tilapia

(Prepping time: 10 minutes| Cooking Time: 4 hours |Serves: 4)

Prepping Time: 10 mins

Cooking Time: 4 hours

Number of Serves: 4

**Ingredients**:

- ½ cup Parmesan cheese, grated

- ¼ cup mayonnaise
- ¼ cup fresh lemon juice
- Salt and ground black pepper, as required
- 4 (4-ounce) tilapia fillets
- 2 tablespoons fresh cilantro, chopped

**Preparation:**

1. In a bowl, mix together all ingredients except tilapia fillets and cilantro.
2. Coat the fillets with mayonnaise mixture evenly.
3. Place the filets over a large piece of foil.
4. Wrap the foil around fillets to seal them.
5. Arrange the foil packet in the bottom of Ninja Foodi.
6. Close the Ninja Foodi with crisping lid and select "Slow Cooker".
7. Set on "Low" for 3-4 hours.
8. Press "Start/Stop" to begin cooking.
9. Open the lid and transfer the foil parcel onto a platter.
10. Carefully open the parcel and serve hot with the garnishing of cilantro.

**Nutritional Information Per Serving:**

Calories: 190, Fat: 8.5 g, Saturated Fat: 2.5 g, Trans Fat: 6 g, Carbohydrates: 3.9 g, Fiber 0.1 g, Sodium 237 mg, Protein: 25.4 g

# Cherry Tomato Mackerel

(Prepping time: 10 minutes| Cooking Time: 7 minutes |Serves: 4)

**Ingredients:**

- 4 Mackerel fillets
- ¼ teaspoon onion powder
- ¼ teaspoon lemon powder
- ¼ teaspoon garlic powder
- ½ teaspoon salt
- 2 cups cherry tomatoes
- 3 tablespoons melted butter
- 1 and ½ cups of water
- 1 tablespoon black olives

**Preparation:**

1. Take a baking dish and grease it well
2. Arrange cherry tomatoes at the bottom of the dish
3. Top with fillets sprinkle listed spices

4. Drizzle melted butter on top

5. Add water to the Ninja Foodi, lower rack in Foodi and place the baking dish

6. Lock lid and cook on LOW Pressure for 7 minutes

7. Quick-release, the Pressure, stay cautious

8. Serve and enjoy!

**Nutritional Information Per Serving:**

Calories: 325, Fat: 24g, Saturated Fat: 5 g, Carbohydrates: 2 g, Fiber: 3 g, Sodium: 964 mg, Protein: 21 g

# Glazed Haddock

(Prepping time: 15 minutes| Cooking Time: 11 minutes |Serves: 4)

**Ingredients:**

- 1 garlic clove, minced
- ¼ teaspoon fresh ginger, grated finely
- ½ cup low-sodium soy sauce
- ¼ cup fresh lime juice
- ½ cup chicken broth
- ¼ cup sugar
- ¼ teaspoon red pepper flakes, crushed
- 1 pound haddock steak

**Preparation:**

1. Select "Sauté/Sear" setting of Ninja Foodi and place all ingredients except haddock steak.

2. Press "Start/Stop" to begin and cook for about 3-4 minutes, stirring continuously.

3. Press "Start/Stop" to stop cooking and transfer the mixture into a bowl.

4. Set aside to cool.

5. In a bowl, reserve half of the marinade.

6. In a resealable bag, add the remaining marinade and haddock steak.

7. Seal the bag and shake to coat well.

8. Refrigerate for about 30 minutes.

9. Arrange the greased "Cook & Crisp Basket" in the pot of Ninja Foodi.

10. Close the Ninja Foodi with crisping lid and select "Air Crisp".

11. Set the temperature to 390 degrees F for 5 minutes.

12. Press "Start/Stop" to begin preheating.

13. After preheating, open the lid.

14. Place the haddock steak into the "Cook & Crisp Basket".

15. Close the Ninja Foodi with crisping lid and select "Air Crisp".

16. Set the temperature to 390 degrees F for 11 minutes.
17. Press "Start/Stop" to begin cooking.
18. Open the lid and transfer the haddock steak onto a serving platter.
19. Immediately coat the haddock steaks with the remaining glaze.
20. Serve immediately.

**Nutritional Information Per Serving:**

Calories: 192, Fat: 1.2 g, Saturated Fat: 0.2 g, Trans Fat: 1 g, Carbohydrates: 15.1 g, Fiber 0.1 g , Sodium 1090 mg, Protein: 3.2 g

# Scallops with Spinach

(Prepping time: 15 minutes| Cooking Time: 10 minutes |Serves: 3)

**Ingredients:**

- 1 (10-ounce) package frozen spinach, thawed and drained
- 12 sea scallops
- Olive oil cooking spray
- Salt and ground black pepper, as required
- ¾ cup heavy whipping cream
- 1 tablespoon tomato paste
- 1 teaspoon garlic, minced
- 1 tablespoon fresh basil, chopped

**Preparation:**

1. Arrange the greased "Cook & Crisp Basket" in the pot of Ninja Foodi.
2. Close the Ninja Foodi with crisping lid and select "Air Crisp".
3. Set the temperature to 350 degrees F for 5 minutes.
4. Press "Start/Stop" to begin preheating.
5. In the bottom of a 7-inch heatproof pan, place the spinach.
6. Spray each scallop with cooking spray and then sprinkle with a little salt and black pepper.
7. Arrange scallops on top of the spinach in a single layer.
8. In a bowl, add the cream, tomato paste, garlic, basil, salt and black pepper and mix well.
9. Place the cream mixture over the spinach and scallops evenly.
10. After preheating, open the lid.
11. Place the pan into "Cook & Crisp Basket".
12. Close the Ninja Foodi with crisping lid and select "Air Crisp".
13. Set the temperature to 350 degrees F for 10 minutes.
14. Press "Start/Stop" to begin cooking.
15. Open the lid and serve hot.

**Nutritional Information Per Serving:**

Calories: 237, Fat: 12.4 g, Saturated Fat: 7.1 g, Trans Fat: 5.3 g, Carbohydrates: 8.4 g, Fiber 2.3 g, Sodium 335 mg, Protein: 23.8 g

# Cod Parcel

(Prepping time: 15 minutes| Cooking Time: 8 minutes |Serves: 2)

**Ingredients**:

- 2 (4-ounce) cod fillets
- ½ teaspoon garlic powder
- Salt and ground black pepper, as required
- 2 fresh dill sprigs
- 4 lemon slices
- 2 tablespoons butter

**Preparation:**

1. Arrange 2 large parchment squares onto a smooth surface.

2. Place 1 fillet in the center of each parchment square and sprinkle with garlic powder, salt and black pepper.

3. Top each fillet with 1 dill sprig, 2 lemon slices and 1 tablespoon of butter.

4. Fold each parchment paper around the fillets to seal.

5. In the pot of Ninja Foodi, place 1 cup of water.

6. Arrange the "Reversible Rack" in the pot of Ninja Foodi.

7. Place the fish parcels over the "Reversible Rack".

8. Close the Ninja Foodi with the pressure lid and place the pressure valve to "Seal" position.

9. Select "Pressure" and set to "High for 8 minutes.

10. Press "Start/Stop" to begin cooking.

11. Switch the valve to "Vent" and do a "Quick" release.

12. Open the lid and transfer the fish parcels onto serving plates.

13. Carefully unwrap the parcels and serve.

**Nutritional Information Per Serving:**

Calories: 227, Fat: 12.9 g, Saturated Fat: 7.3 g, Trans Fat: 5.6 g, Carbohydrates: 10.3 g, Fiber 3 g, Sodium 234 mg, Protein: 21.8 g

# Garlic Flavored Prawn Meal

(Prepping time: 5 minutes| Cooking Time: 5 minutes |Serves: 4)

**Ingredients:**

- 1 pound prawns
- 2/3 cup fish stock
- 1 tablespoon butter
- 2 tablespoons olive oil
- 2 tablespoons garlic, minced
- 2 tablespoons lemon juice
- 1 tablespoon lemon zest
- Salt and pepper to taste

**Preparation:**

1. Set your Ninja Foodi to Saute mode
2. Add oil and butter, let it heat up
3. Stir in remaining ingredients
4. Close the lid
5. Cook for 5 minutes on LOW
6. Quick-release the Pressure
7. Serve and enjoy!

**Nutritional Information Per Serving:**

Calories: 236, Fat: 12g, Saturated Fat: 3 g, Carbohydrates: 2g, Fiber: 1 g, Sodium: 964 mg, Protein: 27g


# Simple Salmon Stew

(Prepping time: 10-60 minutes| Cooking Time: 5-10 minutes |Serves: 4)

**Ingredients:**

- 1 cup fish broth
- Salt and pepper to taste
- 1 medium onion, chopped
- 1-2 pounds salmon fillets, cubed
- 1 tablespoon butter

**Preparation:**

1. Take a large-sized bowl and add shrimp, alongside listed ingredients
2. Let them sit for 30 -50 minutes
3. Take your inner pot and grease it well, add butter and transfer the marinated shrimp to the pot
4. Lock lid and cook on BAKE/ROAST mode for 15 minutes at 355 degrees F

5. Open the lid, serve, and enjoy!

**Nutritional Information Per Serving:**

Calories: 173, Fat: 8g, Saturated Fat: 2 g, Carbohydrates: 0.1 g, Fiber: 0 g, Sodium: mg, Protein: 23 g

# Seafood & Tomato Stew

(Prepping time: 10 minutes| Cooking Time: 4 hours 50 minutes |Serves: 8)

**Ingredients:**

- 2 tablespoons olive oil
- 1 pound tomatoes, chopped
- 1 large yellow onion, chopped finely
- 2 garlic cloves, minced
- 2 teaspoons curry powder
- 6 sprigs fresh parsley
- Salt and ground black pepper, as required
- 1½ cups chicken broth
- 1½ pounds salmon, cut into cubes
- 1½ pounds shrimp, peeled and deveined

**Preparation:**

1. In the pot of Ninja Foodi, add all ingredients except seafood and mix well.
2. Close the Ninja Foodi with crisping lid and select "Slow Cooker".
3. Set on "High" for 4 hours.
4. Press "Start/Stop" to begin cooking.
5. Open the lid and stir in the seafood.
6. Now, set on "Low" for 50 minutes.
7. Press "Start/Stop" to begin cooking.
8. Open the lid and serve hot.

**Nutritional Information Per Serving:**

Calories: 272, Fat: 10.7 g, Saturated Fat: 1.8 g, Trans Fat: 8.9 g, Carbohydrates: 6 g, Fiber: 1.3 g, Sodium: 412 mg, Protein: 37.6 g

# Garlic and Lemon Prawn Dish

(Prepping time: 10 minutes| Cooking Time: 5 minutes |Serves: 4)

**Ingredients:**

- 2 tablespoons olive oil
- 1 pound prawns

- 2 tablespoons garlic, minced
- 2/3 cup fish stock
- 1 tablespoon butter
- 2 tablespoons lemon juice
- 1 tablespoon lemon zest
- Salt and pepper to taste

**Preparation:**

1. Set your Ninja Food to Saute mode
2. Let it heat up, add butter and oil
3. Stir in rest of the listed ingredients
4. Lock lid and cook on LOW Pressure for 5 minutes
5. Quick-release the Pressure
6. Serve and enjoy!

**Nutritional Information Per Serving:**

Calories: 236, Fat: 12g, Saturated Fat: 12 g, Carbohydrates: 2 g, Fiber: 3 g, Sodium: mg, Protein: 27 g

# Shrimp Zoodles

(Prepping time: 5 minutes| Cooking Time: 3 minutes |Serves: 4)

**Ingredients:**

- 4 cups zoodles
- 1 tablespoon basil, chopped
- 2 tablespoons Ghee
- 1 cup vegetable stock
- 2 garlic cloves, minced
- 2 tablespoons olive oil
- ½ lemon
- ½ teaspoon paprika

**Preparation:**

1. Set your Ninja Foodi to Saute mode and add ghee, let it heat up
2. Add olive oil as well
3. Add garlic and cook for 1 minute
4. Add lemon juice, shrimp and cook for 1 minute
5. Stir in rest of the ingredients and lock lid, cook on LOW Pressure for 5 minutes
6. Quick-release Pressure and serve
7. Enjoy!

**Nutritional Information Per Serving:**

Calories: 227, Fat: 6g, Saturated Fat: 2 g, Carbohydrates: 5g, Fiber: 2 g, Sodium: 964 mg, Protein: 27g

# Buttered Crab Legs

(Prepping time: 15 minutes| Cooking Time: 4 minutes |Serves: 2)

**Ingredients:**

- 1½ pounds frozen crab legs
- Salt, as required
- 2 tablespoons butter, melted

**Preparation:**

1. In the pot of Ninja Foodi, place 1 cup of water and 1 teaspoon of salt.
2. Arrange the "Reversible Rack" in the pot of Ninja Foodi.
3. Place the crab legs over the "Reversible Rack "and sprinkle with salt.
4. Close the Ninja Foodi with the pressure lid and place the pressure valve to "Seal" position.
5. Select "Pressure" and set to "High" for 4 minutes.
6. Press "Start/Stop" to begin cooking.
7. Switch the valve to "Vent" and do a "Quick" release.
8. Open the lid and transfer crab legs onto a serving platter.
9. Drizzle with butter and serve.

**Nutritional Information Per Serving:**

Calories: 445, Fat: 16.7 g, Saturated Fat: 7.3 g, Trans Fat: 9.4 g, Carbohydrates: 0 g, Fiber 0 g, Sodium 2009 mg, Protein: 65.4 g

# Shrimp Scampi

(Prepping time: 15 minutes| Cooking Time: 7 minutes |Serves: 3)

**Ingredients:**

- 4 tablespoons salted butter
- 1 tablespoon fresh lemon juice
- 1 tablespoon garlic, minced
- 2 teaspoons red pepper flakes, crushed
- 1 pound shrimp, peeled and deveined
- 2 tablespoons fresh basil, chopped
- 1 tablespoon fresh chives, chopped
- 2 tablespoons chicken broth

**Preparation:**

1. Arrange a 7-inch round baking pan in the "Cook & Crisp Basket".
2. Now, arrange the "Cook & Crisp Basket" in the pot of Ninja Foodi.
3. Close the Ninja Foodi with crisping lid and select "Air Crisp".
4. Set the temperature to 325 degrees F for 5 minutes.
5. Press "Start/Stop" to begin preheating.
6. After preheating, open the lid and carefully remove the pan from Ninja Foodi.
7. In the heated pan, place butter, lemon juice, garlic, and red pepper flakes and mix well.
8. Place the pan in the "Cook & Crisp Basket".
9. Close the Ninja Foodi with crisping lid and select "Air Crisp".
10. Set the temperature to 325 degrees F for 7 minutes.
11. Press "Start/Stop" to begin cooking.
12. After 2 minutes of cooking, stir in the shrimp, basil, chives and broth.
13. Open the lid and place the pan onto a wire rack for about 1 minute.
14. Stir the mixture and serve hot.

**Nutritional Information Per Serving:**

Calories: 245, Fat: 15.7 g, Saturated Fat: 8 g, Trans Fat: 7.7 g, Carbohydrates: 3.1 g, Fiber 0.3 g, Sodium 384 mg, Protein: 26.4 g

# Chapter 5: Vegetarian and Vegan Recipes

## Comfortable Mushroom Soup

(Prepping time: 10 minutes| Cooking Time: 10 minutes |Serves: 6)

**Ingredients**

- 1 small onion, diced
- 8 ounces white button mushrooms, chopped
- 8 ounces portabella mushrooms
- 2 garlic cloves, minced
- ¼ cup dry white wine vinegar
- 2 and ½ cup mushroom stock
- 2 teaspoons salt
- 1 teaspoon fresh thyme
- ¼ teaspoon black pepper

Cashew Cream

- 1/3 cup of raw cashew
- ½ a cup of mushroom stock

**Preparation:**

1. Add onion, mushroom to the pot and set your Ninja Foodi to Saute mode
2. Cook for 8 minutes and stir from time to time
3. Add garlic and Saute for 2 minutes more
4. Add wine and Saute until evaporated
5. Add thyme, pepper, salt, Mushroom stock, and stir
6. Lock up the lid and cook on HIGH pressure for 5 minutes
7. Perform quick release
8. Transfer cashew and water to the blender and blend well
9. Remove lid and transfer mix to the blender
10. Blend until smooth
11. Server and enjoy!

**Nutritional Information Per Serving:**

Calories: 193, Fats: 12g, Carbs:15g, Protein: 5

# Beets and Greens with Cool Horseradish Sauce

(Prepping time: 5 minutes| Cooking Time: 10-15 minutes |Serves: 4)

## Ingredients

- 2 large beets with greens, scrubbed and root ends trimmed
- 1 cup water, for steaming
- 2 tablespoons sour cream
- 1 tablespoon almond milk
- 1 teaspoon prepared horseradish
- ¼ teaspoon lemon zest
- 1/8 teaspoon salt
- 2 teaspoon unsalted butter
- 1 tablespoon minced fresh chives

## Preparation:

1. Trim off beet greens and keep them on the side
2. Add water to the Ninja Foodi and place steamer basket, place beets in steamer basket
3. Lock lid and cook on HIGH pressure for 10 minutes, release pressure naturally over 10 minutes
4. While the beets are being cooked, wash greens and slice them into ½ inch thick ribbons
5. Take a bowl and whisk in sour cream, horseradish, lemon zest, 1/16 teaspoon of salt
6. Once the cooking is done, remove lid and remove beets, let them cool
7. Use a pairing knife to peel them and slice them into large bite-sized pieces
8. Remove steamer from the Ninja Foodi and pour out water
9. Set your Foodi to "Saute" mode and add butter, let it melt
10. Once the butter stops foaming, add beet greens sprinkle remaining 1/6 teaspoon salt and cook for 3-4 minutes
11. Return beets to the Foodi and heat for 1-2 minutes, stirring
12. Transfer beets and greens to platter and drizzle sour cream mixture
13. Sprinkle chives and serve. Enjoy!

## Nutritional Information Per Serving:

Calories: 70, Fat: 4g, Carbohydrates: 9g, Protein: 2g


# Garlic and Dill Carrot Fiesta

(Prepping time: 5 minutes| Cooking Time: 12 minutes |Serves: 4)

## Ingredients

- 3 cups carrots, chopped
- 1 tablespoon melted butter
- ½ teaspoon garlic sea salt

- 1 tablespoon fresh dill, minced
- 1 cup water

**Preparation:**

1. Add listed ingredients to Ninja Foodi
2. Stir and lock lid, cook on HIGH pressure for 10 minutes
3. Release pressure naturally over 10 minutes
4. Quick release pressure and remove lid
5. Serve with a topping of dill, enjoy!

**Nutritional Information Per Serving:**

Calories: 207, Fat: 16g, Carbohydrates: 5g, Protein: 8g

# Healthy Rosemary and Celery Dish

(Prepping time: 10 minutes| Cooking Time: 5 minutes |Serves: 4)

**Ingredients**

- 1 pound celery, cubed
- 1 cup of water
- 2 garlic cloves, minced
- Salt and pepper
- ¼ teaspoon dry rosemary
- 1 tablespoon olive oil

**Preparation:**

1. Add water to your Ninja Foodi and place steamer basket
2. Add celery cubs to basket and lock lid, cook on HIGH pressure for 4 minutes
3. Quick release pressure
4. Take a bowl and add mix in oil, garlic, and rosemary
5. Whisk well
6. Add steamed celery to the bowl and toss well, spread on a lined baking sheet
7. Broil for 3 minutes using the Air Crisping lid at 250 degrees F
8. Serve and enjoy!

**Nutritional Information Per Serving:**

Calories: 100, Fat: 3g, Carbohydrates: 8g, Protein: 3g

# Summertime Veggie Soup

(Prepping time: 10 minutes| Cooking Time: 3 minutes |Serves: 6)

## Ingredients

- 3 cups leeks, sliced
- 6 cups rainbow chard, stems and leaves, chopped
- 1 cup celery, chopped
- 2 tablespoons garlic, minced
- 1 teaspoon dried oregano
- 1 teaspoon salt
- 2 teaspoons fresh ground black pepper
- 3 cups chicken broth
- 2 cups yellow summer squash, sliced into 1/ inch slices
- ¼ cup fresh parsley, chopped
- ¾ cup heavy whip cream
- 4-6 tablespoons parmesan cheese, grated

## Preparation:

1. Add leeks, chard, celery, 1 tablespoon garlic, oregano, salt, pepper and broth to your Ninja Foodi
2. Lock lid and cook on HIGH pressure for 3 minutes
3. Quick release pressure
4. Open lid and add more broth, set your pot to Saute mode and adjust heat to HIGH
5. Add yellow squash, parsley and remaining 1 tablespoon garlic
6. Let it cook for 2-3 minutes until the squash is soft
7. Stir in cream and sprinkle parmesan
8. Serve and enjoy!

## Nutritional Information Per Serving:

Calories: 210, Fat: 14g, Carbohydrates: 10g, Protein: 10g

# Astounding Caramelized Onions

(Prepping time: 10 minutes| Cooking Time: 45 minutes |Serves: 4)

## Ingredients

- 2 tablespoons unsalted butter
- 3 large onions, sliced
- 2 tablespoons water
- 1 teaspoon salt

## Preparation:

1. Set your pot to Saute mode and adjust the heat to Medium, pre-heat the inner pot for 5 minutes

2. Add butter and let it melt, add onions, water, salt, and stir well

3. Lock pressure lid into place, making sure that the pressure valve is locked

4. Cook on HIGH pressure for 30 minutes

5. Quick release the pressure once done

6. Remove the lid and set the pot to Saute mode, let it sear in the Medium-HIGH mode for about 15 minutes until the liquid is almost gone

7. Enjoy!

**Nutritional Information Per Serving:**

Calories: 110, Fat: 6g, Carbohydrates: 10g, Protein: 2g

# Cool Indian Palak Paneer

(Prepping time: 10 minutes| Cooking Time: 5 minutes |Serves: 4)

**Ingredients**

- 2 teaspoons olive oil
- 5 garlic cloves, chopped
- 1 tablespoon fresh ginger, chopped
- 1 large yellow onion, chopped
- ½ jalapeno chile, chopped
- 1 pound fresh spinach
- 2 tomatoes, chopped
- 2 teaspoons ground cumin
- ½ teaspoon cayenne
- 2 teaspoons Garam masala
- 1 teaspoon ground turmeric
- 1 teaspoon salt
- ½ cup water
- 1 and ½ cup paneer cubes
- ½ cup heavy whip cream

**Preparation:**

1. Pre-heat your Ninja Foodi using Saute mode on HIGH heat, once the pot is hot, add oil and let it shimmer

2. Add garlic, ginger and chile, Saute for 2-3 minutes

3. Add onion, spinach, tomatoes, cumin, cayenne, garam masala, turmeric, salt and water

4. Lock lid and cook on HIGH pressure for 2 minutes

5. Release pressure naturally over 10 minutes

6. Use an immersion blender to puree the mixture to your desired consistency

7.  Gently stir in paneer and top with a drizzle of cream. Enjoy!

**Nutritional Information Per Serving:**

Calories: 185, Fat: 14g, Carbohydrates: 7g, Protein: 7g

# Offbeat Cauliflower and Cheddar Soup

(Prepping time: 10 minutes| Cooking Time: 5 minutes |For 8 servings)

## Ingredients

*   ¼ cup butter
*   ½ sweet onion, chopped
*   1 head cauliflower, chopped
*   4 cups herbed vegetable stock
*   ½ teaspoon ground nutmeg
*   1 cup heavy whip cream
*   Salt and pepper as needed
*   1 cup cheddar cheese, shredded

## Preparation:

1.  Set your Ninja Foodi to sauté mode and add butter , let it heat up and melt
2.  Add onion and Cauliflower, Saute for 10 minutes until tender and lightly browned
3.  Add vegetable stock and nutmeg, bring to a boil
4.  Lock lid and cook on HIGH pressure for 5 minutes, quick release pressure once done
5.  Remove pot and from Foodi and stir in heavy cream, puree using immersion blender
6.  Season with more salt and pepper and serve with a topping of cheddar
7.  Enjoy!

**Nutritional Information Per Serving:**

Calories: 227, Fat: 21g, Carbohydrates: 4g, Protein: 8g

# Groovy Broccoli Florets

(Prepping time: 10 minutes| Cooking Time: 6 minutes |Serves: 4)

## Ingredients

*   4 tablespoons butter, melted
*   Salt and pepper to taste
*   2 pounds broccoli florets
*   1 cup whipping cream

## Preparation:

1.  Place a steamer basket in your Ninja Foodi (bottom part) and add water
2.  Place florets on top of the basket and lock lid

3. Cook on HIGH pressure for 5 minutes

4. Quick release pressure

5. Transfer florets from the steamer basket to the pot

6. Add salt, pepper, butter and stir

7. Lock crisping lid and cook on Air Crisp mode for 360 degrees F

8. Serve and enjoy!

**Nutritional Information Per Serving:**

Calories: 178, Fat: 14g, Carbohydrates: 8g, Protein: 5g

# Cheese Dredged Cauliflower Delight

(Prepping time: 5 minutes| Cooking Time: 30 minutes |Serves: 6)

## Ingredients

• 1 tablespoon Keto-Friendly mustard

• 1 head cauliflower

• 1 teaspoon avocado mayonnaise

• ½ cup parmesan cheese, grated

• ¼ cup butter, cut into small pieces

## Preparation:

1. Set your Ninja Foodi to Saute mode and add butter, let it melt

2. Add cauliflower and Saute for 3 minutes

3. Add remaining ingredients and lock lid

4. Cook on PRESSURE mode for 30 minutes on HIGH pressure

5. Release pressure natural over 10 minutes

6. Serve and enjoy!

**Nutritional Information Per Serving:**

Calories: 155, Fat: 13g, Carbohydrates: 2g, Protein: 7g

# Creative Coconut Cabbage

(Prepping time: 10 minutes | Cooking Time: 7 minutes |Serves: 4)

## Ingredients

• 2 tablespoons lemon juice

• 1/3 medium carrot, sliced

• ½ ounces, yellow onion, sliced

• 1/2 cup cabbage, shredded

• 1 teaspoon turmeric powder

• 1 ounce dry coconut

- ½ tablespoon mustard powder
- ½ teaspoon mild curry powder
- 1 large garlic cloves, diced
- 1 and ½ teaspoons salt
- 1/3 cup water
- 3 tablespoons olive oil
- 3 large whole eggs
- 3 large egg yolks

**Preparation:**

1. Set your Ninja Foodi to Saute mode and add oil, stir in onions, salt and cook for 4 minutes
2. Stir in spices, garlic and Saute for 30 seconds
3. Stir in rest of the ingredients, lock lid and cook on HIGH pressure for 3 minutes
4. Naturally, release pressure over 10 minutes
5. Serve and enjoy!

**Nutritional Information Per Serving:**

Calories: 400, Fat: 34g, Carbohydrates: 10g, Protein: 14g

# Awesome Veggie Hash

(Prepping time: 10 minutes | Cooking Time: 15 minutes |Serves: 4)

**Ingredients**

- 1 cups cauliflower, chopped
- 1 teaspoon mustard
- ½ cup dark leaf kale, chopped
- 1 tablespoon lemon juice
- ½ cup spinach, chopped
- ½ teaspoon salt
- 2 garlic cloves
- ½ teaspoon pepper
- 6 whole eggs
- 3 teaspoons coconut oil

**Preparation:**

1. Set your Ninja Foodi to Saute mode and add coconut oil, add garlic, cook until fragrant
2. Add chopped cauliflower and cook for 5 minutes
3. Stir in all ingredients except eggs, cook for 2 minutes
4. Stir in eggs, lock lid and cook for 2 minutes on HIGH pressure
5. Quick release pressure

6.  Enjoy!

**Nutritional Information Per Serving:**

Calories: 480, Fat: 35g, Carbohydrates: 8g, Protein: 22g

# Garlic and Swiss Chard Garlic

(Prepping time: 10 minutes | Cooking Time: 4 minutes |Serves: 4)

**Ingredients**

- 2 tablespoons ghee
- 3 tablespoons lemon juice
- ½ cup chicken stock
- 4 bacon slices, chopped
- 1 bunch Swiss chard, chopped
- ½ teaspoon garlic paste
- Salt and pepper to taste

**Preparation:**

1.  Set your Ninja Foodi to Saute mode and add bacon, stir well and cook for a few minutes
2.  Add ghee, lemon juice, garlic paste, and stir
3.  Add Swiss chard, salt, pepper, and stock
4.  Lock lid and cook on HIGH pressure for 3 minutes
5.  Quick release pressure and serve
6.  Enjoy!

**Nutritional Information Per Serving:**

Calories: 160, Fat: 8g, Carbohydrates: 6g, Protein: 4g

# Ginger and Butternut Bisque Yum

(Prepping time: 10 minutes| Cooking Time: 8 minutes |Serves: 6)

**Ingredients**

- 1 cup of diced yellow onion
- 4 minced cloves of garlic
- 2 teaspoon of peeled and chopped ginger
- 1 cup of chopped carrot
- 1 green apple chopped
- 1 peeled and chopped butternut squash
- 1 teaspoon salt
- 2 cups of water
- ¼ cup of finely chopped parsley

- Black pepper

**Preparation:**

1. Prepare the ingredients accordingly and keep them on the side
2. Set your Ninja Foodie to Saute mode and add onions, cook for minutes
3. Add just a splash of water
4. Add garlic, carrot, ginger, apple, squash, and salt
5. Give it a nice stir
6. Add water and lock up the lid
7. Cook on HIGH pressure for 5 minutes
8. Naturally, release the pressure
9. Allow it to cool for 15 minutes
10. Blend the soup in batches, or you may use an immersion blender as well to blend in the pot until it is creamy
11. Add parsley and season with some black pepper
12. Serve and enjoy!

**Nutritional Information Per Serving:**

Protein: 3g, Carbs: 14g, Fats: 5g, Calories: 116

# Complete Cauliflower Zoodles

(Prepping time: 10 minutes| Cooking Time: 8 minutes |Serves: 6)

**Ingredients**

- 2 tablespoons butter
- 2 cloves garlic
- 7-8 cauliflower florets
- 1 cup vegetable broth
- 2 teaspoons salt
- 2 cups spinach, coarsely chopped
- 2 green onions, chopped
- 1 pound of zoodles (Spiralized Zucchini)

**Garnish**

- Chopped sun-dried tomatoes
- Balsamic vinegar
- Gorgonzola cheese

**Preparation:**

1. Set your Ninja Foodi to Saute mode and add butter, allow the butter to melt
2. Add garlic cloves and Saute for 2 minutes

3. Add cauliflower, broth, salt and lock up the lid and cook on HIGH pressure for 6 minutes

4. Prepare the zoodles

5. Perform a naturally release over 10 minutes

6. Use an immersion blender to blend the mixture in the pot to a puree

7. Pour the sauce over the zoodles

8. Serve with a garnish of cheese, sun-dried tomatoes and a drizzle of balsamic vinegar

9. Enjoy!

**Nutritional Information Per Serving:**

Calories: 78, Fats: 5g, Carbs 0.6g, Protein:8g

# Powerful Medi-Cheese Spinach

(Prepping time: 5 minutes| Cooking Time: 15 minutes |Serves: 4)

## Ingredients

- 4 tablespoons butter

- 2 pounds spinach, chopped and boiled

- Salt and pepper to taste

- 2/3 cup Kalamata olives, halved and pitted

- 1 and ½ cups feta cheese, grated

- 4 teaspoons fresh lemon zest, grated

## Preparation:

1. Take a bowl and mix spinach, butter, salt, pepper and transfer the mixture to your Crisping Basket of the Ninja Foodi

2. Transfer basket to your Foodi and lock Crisping lid

3. Cook for 15 minutes on Air Crisp mode on 340 degrees F

4. Serve by stirring in olives, lemon zest and feta

5. Enjoy!

**Nutritional Information Per Serving:**

Calories: 274, Fat: 18g, Carbohydrates: 6g, Protein: 10g

# Thyme and Carrot Dish with Dill

(Prepping time: 5 minutes| Cooking Time: 5 minutes |Serves: 4)

## Ingredients

- ½ cup of water

- 1 pound baby carrots

- 3 tablespoons stevia

- 1 tablespoon thyme, chopped

- 1 tablespoon dill, chopped
- Salt and pepper to taste
- 2 tablespoons ghee

**Preparation:**

1. Add trivet to your Ninja Foodi, add carrots and add water
2. Lock lid and cook on HIGH pressure for 3 minutes
3. Quick release pressure
4. Drain and transfer to a bowl
5. Set your Ninja Foodi to Saute mode and add ghee, let it melt
6. Add stevia, thyme dill, and carrots
7. Stir well for a few minutes
8. Serve and enjoy!

**Nutritional Information Per Serving:**

Calories: 162, Fat: 4g, Carbohydrates: 8g, Protein: 3g

# Delicious Mushroom Stroganoff

(Prepping time: 5 minutes| Cooking Time: 10 minutes |Serves: 6)

**Ingredients**

- ¼ cup unsalted butter, cubed
- 1 pound cremini mushrooms, halved
- 1 large onion, halved
- 4 garlic cloves, minced
- 2 cups vegetable broth
- ½ teaspoon salt
- ¼ teaspoon fresh black pepper
- 1 and ½ cups sour cream
- ¼ cup fresh flat-leaf parsley, chopped
- 1 cup grated parmesan cheese

**Preparation:**

1. Add butter, mushrooms, onion, garlic, vegetable broth, salt, pepper and paprika
2. Gently stir and lock lid
3. Cook on HIGH pressure for 5 minutes
4. Release pressure naturally over 10 minutes
5. Serve by stirring in sour cream and with a garnish of parsley and parmesan cheese
6. Enjoy!

**Nutritional Information Per Serving:**

Calories: 453, Fat: 37g, Carbohydrates: 11g, Protein: 19g

# Chives and Radishes Platter

(Prepping time: 10 minutes| Cooking Time: 7 minutes |Serves: 4)

## Ingredients

- 2 cups radishes, quartered
- ½ cup chicken stock
- Salt and pepper to taste
- 2 tablespoons melted ghee
- 1 tablespoon chives, chopped
- 1 tablespoon lemon zest, grated

## Preparation:

1. Add radishes, stock, salt, pepper, zest to your Ninja Foodi and stir
2. Lock lid and cook on HIGH pressure for 7 minutes
3. Quick release pressure
4. Add melted ghee, toss well
5. Sprinkle chives and enjoy!

## Nutritional Information Per Serving:

Calories: 102, Fat: 4g, Carbohydrates: 6g, Protein: 5g

# Everyday Use Veggie-Stock

(Prepping time: 10 minutes| Cooking Time: 100 minutes |For 1 quart)

## Ingredients

- 1 onion, quartered
- 2 large carrots, peeled and cut into 1 inch pieces
- 1 tablespoon olive oil
- 12 ounces mushrooms, sliced
- ¼ teaspoon salt
- 3 and ½ cups water

## Preparation:

1. Take cook and crisp basket out of the inner pot, close crisping lid and let it pre-heat for 3 minutes at 400 degrees F on Bake/Roast settings

2. While the pot heats up, add onion, carrot chunks in the Cook and Crisp basket and drizzle vegetable oil, toss well

3. Place basket back into the inner pot, close crisping lid and cook for 15 minutes at 400 degrees F on Bake/Roast mode

4. Make sure to shake the basket halfway through

5. Remove basket from pot and add onions, carrots, mushrooms, water and season with salt

6. Lock pressure lid and seal the valves, cook on HIGH pressure for 60 minutes

7. Release the pressure naturally over 10 minutes

8. Line a colander with cheesecloth and place it over a large bowl, pour vegetables and stock into the colander

9. Strain the stock and discard veggies

10. Enjoy and use as needed!

**Nutritional Information Per Serving:**

Calories: 45, Fat: 4g, Carbohydrates: 3g, Protein: 0g

# Special Lunch-Worthy Green Beans

(Prepping time: 5 minutes| Cooking Time: 10 minutes |Serves: 4)

**Ingredients**

- 2-3 pounds fresh green beans

- 2 tablespoons butter

- 1 garlic clove, minced

- Salt and pepper to taste

- 1 and ½ cups water

**Preparation:**

1. Add all listed ingredients to your Ninja Foodi pot

2. Lock lid and cook on HIGH pressure for 5 minutes

3. Release pressure quickly and serve

4. Enjoy!

**Nutritional Information Per Serving:**

Calories: 87, Fat: 6g, Carbohydrates: 7g, Protein: 3g

# Simple Mushroom Hats and Eggs

(Prepping time: 10 minutes| Cooking Time: 9 minutes |For 1 serving)

**Ingredients**

- 4 ounces mushroom hats

- 1 teaspoon butter, melted

- 4 quail eggs

- ½ teaspoon ground black pepper

- ¼ teaspoon salt

**Preparation:**

1. Spread the mushroom hats with the butter inside
2. Then beat the eggs into mushroom hats
3. Sprinkle with salt and ground black pepper
4. Transfer the mushroom hats on the rack
5. Lower the air fryer lid
6. Cook the meat for 7 minutes at 365 F
7. Check the mushroom, if it is not cooked fully then cook them for 2 minutes more
8. Serve and enjoy!

**Nutritional Information Per Serving:**

Calories: 118, Fat: 8.2g, Carbohydrates: 4.6g, Protein: 8.4g

# Healthy Cauliflower Mash

(Prepping time: 10 minutes| Cooking Time: 5 minutes |Serves: 4)

## Ingredients

- 1 tablespoon butter, soft
- ½ cup feta cheese
- Salt and pepper to taste
- 1 large head cauliflower, chopped into large pieces
- 1 garlic cloves, minced
- 2 teaspoons fresh chives, minced

## Preparation:

1. Add the pot to your Ninja Foodi and add water
2. Add steamer basket on top and add cauliflower pieces
3. Lock lid and cook on HIGH pressure for 5 minutes
4. Quick release pressure
5. Open lid and use an immersion blender to mash the cauliflower
6. Blend until you have your desired consistency and enjoy!

**Nutritional Information Per Serving:**

Calories: 124, Fat: 10g, Carbohydrates: 5g, Protein: 5g

# Awesome Butternut Squash Soup

(Prepping time: 10 minutes| Cooking Time: 16 minutes |Serves: 4)

## Ingredients

- 1 and ½ pounds butternut squash, baked, peeled and cubed
- ½ cup green onions, chopped
- 3 tablespoons butter

- ½ cup carrots, peeled and chopped
- ½ cup celery, chopped
- 29 ounces vegetable stock
- 1 garlic clove, peeled and minced
- ½ teaspoon Italian seasoning
- 15 ounces canned tomatoes, diced
- Salt and pepper to taste
- 1/8 teaspoon red pepper flakes
- 1/8 teaspoon nutmeg, grated
- 1 and ½ cup half and half

**Preparation:**

1. Set your Ninja Foodi to "Saute" mode and add butter, let it melt
2. Add celery, carrots, onion and stir cook for 3 minutes
3. Add garlic, stir cook for 1 minute
4. Add squash, tomatoes, stock, Italian seasoning, salt, pepper, pepper flakes and nutmeg, stir
5. Lock lid and cook on HIGH pressure for 10 minutes
6. Release pressure naturally over 10 minutes
7. Use an immersion blender to puree the mix
8. Set the food to Saute mode on LOW and add half and half, stir cook for 1-2 minutes until thickened
9. Divide and serve with a sprinkle of green onions on top
10. Enjoy!

**Nutritional Information Per Serving:**

Calories: 250, Fat: 22g, Carbohydrates: 8g, Protein: 3g

# Chapter 6: Snacks and Appetizers Recipes

## Simple Treat of Garlic

(Prepping time: 10 minutes | Cooking Time: 5 minutes |Serves: 4)

**Ingredients:**

- 1 tablespoon extra-virgin olive oil
- 2 garlic cloves, minced
- 2 large-sized Belgian endive, halved lengthwise
- ½ cup apple cider vinegar
- ½ cup broth
- Salt and pepper to taste
- 1 teaspoon cayenne pepper

**Preparation:**

1. Set your Ninja Foodi to Saute mode and add oil, let the oil heat up
2. Add garlic and cook for 30 seconds unto browned
3. Add endive, vinegar, broth, salt, pepper, and cayenne
4. Lock lid and cook on LOW pressure for 2 minutes. Quick release pressure and serve. Enjoy!

**Nutritional Information Per Serving:**

Calories: 91, Fat: 6g, Carbohydrates: 3g, Protein: 2g

## Cauliflower and Egg Dish

(Prepping time: 10 minutes | Cooking Time: 4 minutes |Serves: 4)

**Ingredients:**

- 21 ounces cauliflower, separated into florets
- 1 cup red onion, chopped
- 1 cup celery, chopped
- ½ cup of water
- Salt and pepper to taste
- 2 tablespoons balsamic vinegar
- 1 teaspoon stevia
- 4 boiled eggs, chopped
- 1 cup Keto Friendly mayonnaise

**Preparation:**

1. Add water to Ninja Foodi
2. Add steamer basket and add cauliflower, lock lid and cook on High Pressure for 5 minutes

3. Quick release pressure. Transfer cauliflower to bowl and add eggs, celery, onion and toss

4. Take another bowl and mix in mayo, salt, pepper, vinegar, stevia and whisk well

5. Add a salad, toss well. Divide into salad bowls and serve. Enjoy!

**Nutritional Information Per Serving:**

Calories: 170, Fat: 4g, Carbohydrates: 5g, Protein: 5g

# The Original Zucchini Gratin

(Prepping time: 10 minutes| Cooking Time: 15 minutes |Serves: 4)

**Ingredients:**

- 2 zucchinis
- 1 tablespoon fresh parsley, chopped
- 2 tablespoons bread crumbs
- 4 tablespoons parmesan cheese, grated
- 1 tablespoon vegetable oil
- Salt and pepper to taste

**Preparation:**

1. Pre-heat your Ninja Foodi to 300 degrees F for 3 minutes

2. Slice zucchini lengthwise to get about 8 equal sizes pieces

3. Arrange pieces in your Crisping Basket (skin side down)

4. Top each with parsley, bread crumbs, cheese, oil, salt, and pepper

5. Return basket Ninja Foodi basket and cook for 15 minutes at 360 degrees F

6. Once done, serve with sauce. Enjoy!

**Nutritional Information Per Serving:**

Calories: 481, Fat: 11g, Carbohydrates: 10g, Protein: 7g

# Spaghetti Squash and Chicken Parmesan

(Prepping time: 10 minutes| Cooking Time: 20 minutes |Serves: 4)

**Ingredients:**

- 1 spaghetti squash
- 1 cup marinara sauce (Keto Friendly)
- 1 pound chicken, cooked and cubed
- 16 ounces mozzarella

**Preparation:**

1. Split up the squash in halves and remove the seeds

2. Add 1 cup of water to the Ninja Foodi and place a trivet on top

3. Add the squash halves on the trivet. Lock up the lid and cook for 20 minutes at HIGH pressure

4. Do a quick release. Remove the squashes and shred them using a fork into spaghetti portions

5. Pour sauce over the squash and give it a nice mix

6. Top them up with the cubed up chicken and top with mozzarella

7. Broil for 1-2 minutes and broil until the cheese has melted

**Nutritional Information Per Serving:**

Calories: 127, Fats: 8g, Carbs:11g, Protein:5g

# Egg Dredged Casserole

(Prepping time: 10 minutes| Cooking Time: 5 minutes |Serves: 6)

**Ingredients:**

- 4 whole eggs
- 1 tablespoons milk
- 1 tomato, diced
- ½ cup spinach
- ¼ teaspoon salt
- ¼ teaspoon ground black pepper

**Preparation:**

1. Take a baking pan ( small enough to fit Ninja Foodi) and grease it with butter

2. Take a medium bowl and whisk in eggs, milk, salt, pepper, add veggies to the bowl and stir

3. Pour egg mixture into the baking pan and lower the pan into the Ninja Foodi

4. Close Air Crisping lid and Air Crisp for 325 degrees for 7 minutes

5. Remove the pan from eggs and enjoy hot!

**Nutritional Information Per Serving:**

Calories: 78, Fat: 5g, Carbohydrates: 1g, Protein: 7g

# Obvious Paprika and Cabbage

(Prepping time: 10 minutes | Cooking Time: 4 minutes |Serves: 4)

**Ingredients:**

- 1 and ½ pounds green cabbage, shredded
- Salt and pepper to taste
- 3 tablespoon ghee
- 1 cup vegetable stock
- ¼ teaspoon sweet paprika

**Preparation:**

1. Set your Ninja Foodi to Saute mode and add ghee, let it melt

2. Add cabbage, salt, pepper, and stock, stir well

3. Lock lid and cook on HIGH pressure for 7 minutes. Quick release pressure

4. Add paprika and toss well. Divide between plates and serve. Enjoy!

**Nutritional Information Per Serving:**

Calories: 170, Fat: 4g, Carbohydrates: 5g, Protein: 5g

# Buttered Up Garlic and Fennel

(Prepping time: 10 minutes | Cooking Time: 5 minutes |Serves: 4)

**Ingredients:**

- ½ stick butter

- 2 garlic cloves, sliced

- ½ teaspoon salt

- 1 and ½ pounds fennel bulbs, cut into wedges

- ¼ teaspoon ground black pepper

- ½ teaspoon cayenne

- ¼ teaspoon dried dill weed

- 1/3 cup dry white wine

- 2/3 cup stock

**Preparation:**

1. Set your Ninja Foodi to Saute mode and add butter, let it heat up

2. Add garlic and cook for 30 seconds. Add rest of the ingredients

3. Lock lid and cook on LOW pressure for 3 minutes. Remove lid and serve. Enjoy!

**Nutritional Information Per Serving:**

Calories: 111, Fat: 6g, Carbohydrates: 2g, Protein: 2g

# Ultimate Cheese Dredged Cauliflower Snack

(Prepping time: 10 minutes| Cooking Time: 30 minutes |Serves: 4)

**Ingredients:**

- 1 tablespoon mustard

- 1 head cauliflower

- 1 teaspoon avocado mayonnaise

- ½ cup parmesan cheese, grated

- ¼ cup butter, cut into small pieces

**Preparation:**

1. Set your Ninja Foodi to Saute mode and add butter and cauliflower

2. Saute for 3 minutes. Add remaining ingredients and stir

3. Lock lid and cook on HIGH pressure for 30 minutes. Release pressure naturally over 10 minutes

4. Serve and enjoy!

**Nutritional Information Per Serving:**

Calories: 155, Fat: 13g, Carbohydrates: 4g, Protein: 6g

# Juicy Garlic Chicken Livers

(Prepping time: 10 minutes| Cooking Time: 8 hours |Serves: 6)

**Ingredients:**

- 1 pound chicken livers
- 8 garlic cloves, minced
- 8 ounces cremini mushrooms, quartered
- 4 slices uncooked bacon, chopped
- 1 onion, chopped
- 1 cup bone broth
- 1 teaspoon dried thyme
- 1 teaspoon dried rosemary
- 1 teaspoon salt
- 1 teaspoon freshly ground black pepper
- ¼ cup fresh parsley, chopped

**Preparation:**

1. Add livers, bacon, garlic, mushrooms, onion, thyme, broth, rosemary to Ninja Foodi
2. Season with salt and pepper. Place lid and cook on SLOW COOK Mode (LOW) for 8 hours
3. Remove lid and stir in parsley. Serve and enjoy!

**Nutritional Information Per Serving:**

Calories: 210, Fat: 9g, Carbohydrates: 6g, Protein: 24g

# Quick Bite Zucchini Fries

(Prepping time: 10 minutes| Cooking Time: 10 minutes |Serves: 4)

**Ingredients:**

- 1-2 pounds of zucchini, sliced into 2 and ½ inch sticks
- Salt to taste
- 1 cup cream cheese
- 2 tablespoons olive oil

**Preparation:**

1. Add zucchini in a colander and season with salt, add cream cheese and mix
2. Add oil into your Ninja Foodie's pot and add Zucchini
3. Lock Air Crisping Lid and set the temperature to 365 degrees F and timer to 10 minutes

4. Let it cook for 10 minutes and take the dish out once done, enjoy!

**Nutritional Information Per Serving:**

Calories: 374, Fat: 36g, Carbohydrates: 6g, Protein: 7g

# Rise and Shine Breakfast Casserole

(Prepping time: 10 minutes| Cooking Time: 10 minutes |Serves: 6)

**Ingredients:**

- 4 whole eggs
- 1 tablespoons milk
- 1 cup ham, cooked and chopped
- ½ cup cheddar cheese, shredded
- ¼ teaspoon salt
- ¼ teaspoon ground black pepper

**Preparation:**

1. Take a baking pan (small enough to fit into your Ninja Foodi) bowl, and grease it well with butter. Take a medium bowl and whisk in eggs, milk, salt, pepper and add ham, cheese, and stir. Pour mixture into baking pan and lower the pan into your Ninja Foodi

2. Set your Ninja Foodi Air Crisp mode and Air Crisp for 325 degrees F for 7 minutes

3. Remove pan from eggs and enjoy!

**Nutritional Information Per Serving:**

Calories: 169, Fat: 13g, Carbohydrates: 1g, Protein: 12g

# Authentic Western Omelet

(Prepping time: 5 minutes| Cooking Time: 34 minutes |For 2 servings)

**Ingredients:**

- 3 eggs, whisked
- 3 ounces chorizo, chopped
- 1-ounces Feta cheese, crumbled
- 5 tablespoons almond milk
- ¾ teaspoon chili flakes
- ¼ teaspoon salt
- 1 green pepper, chopped

**Preparation:**

1. Add all the ingredients and mix them well. Stir it gently. Take an omelet pan and pour the mixture into it. Preheat your Ninja Foodi at "Roast/Bake" mode at 320 F.

2. Cook for 4 minutes. After that, transfer the pan with an omelet in Ninja Foodi

3. Cook for 30 minutes more at the same mode. Serve hot and enjoy!

**Nutritional Information Per Serving:**

Calories: 426, Fat: 38.2g, Carbohydrates: 6.8g, Protein: 21.7g

# Inspiring Cauliflower Hash Browns

(Prepping time: 10 minutes| Cooking Time: 30 minutes |Serves: 6)

**Ingredients:**

- 6 whole eggs
- 4 cups cauliflower rice
- ¼ cup milk
- 1 onion, chopped
- 3 tablespoons butter
- 1 and ½ cups cooked ham, chopped
- ½ cup shredded cheese

**Preparation:**

1. Set your Ninja Foodi to sauté mode and add butter, let the butter heat up

2. Add onions and cook for 5 minutes until tender. Add iced cauliflower to pot and stir

3. Lock the Air Crisping lid and Air Crisp for 15 minutes, making sure to give them a turn about halfway through

4. Take a small bowl and mix in eggs and milk, pour mixture over browned cauliflower

5. Sprinkle ham over top. Press Air Crispy again and crisp for 10 minutes more

6. Sprinkle cheddar cheese on top and lock lid, let the crisp for 1 minute more until the cheese melts. Serve and enjoy!

**Nutritional Information Per Serving:**

Calories: 166, Fat: 14g, Carbohydrates: 3g, Protein: 9g

# Bowl Full of Broccoli Salad

(Prepping time: 10 minutes | Cooking Time: 5 minutes |Serves: 4)

**Ingredients:**

- 1 pound broccoli, cut into florets
- 2 tablespoons balsamic vinegar
- 2 garlic cloves, minced
- 1 teaspoon mustard seeds
- 1 teaspoon cumin seeds
- Salt and pepper to taste
- 1 cup cottage cheese, crumbled

**Preparation:**

1. Add 1 cup water to your Ninja Foodi. Place steamer basket

2. Place broccoli in basket and lock lid, cook on HIGH pressure for 5 minutes

3. Quick release pressure and remove lid. Toss broccoli with other ingredients and serve. Enjoy!

**Nutritional Information Per Serving:**

Calories: 95, Fat: 3.1g, Carbohydrates: 10g, Protein: 2g

# Pickled Up Green Chili

(Prepping time: 5 minutes| Cooking Time: 11 minutes |Serves: 4)

**Ingredients:**

- 1 pound green chilies
- 1 and ½ cups apple cider vinegar
- 1 teaspoon pickling salt
- 1 and ½ teaspoon sugar
- ¼ teaspoon garlic powder

**Preparation:**

1. Add the listed ingredients to your pot. Lock up the lid and cook on HIGH pressure for 11 minutes. Release the pressure naturally

2. Spoon the mixture into jars and cover the slices with cooking liquid, making sure to completely submerge the chilies. Serve!

**Nutritional Information Per Serving:**

Calories: 3, Fat: 0g, Carbohydrates: 0.8g, Protein: 0.1g

# The Great Mediterranean Spinach

(Prepping time: 10 minutes| Cooking Time: 15 minutes |Serves: 4)

**Ingredients:**

- 4 tablespoons butter
- 2 pounds spinach, chopped and boiled
- Salt and pepper to taste
- 2/3 cup Kalamata olives, halved and pitted
- 1 and ½ cups feta cheese, grated
- 4 teaspoons fresh lemon zest, grated

**Preparation:**

1. Take a bowl and mix in spinach, butter, salt, pepper and mix well

2. Transfer to Ninja Foodi the seasoned spinach

3. Lock Air Crisper and Air Crisp for 15 minutes at 350 degrees F. Serve and enjoy!

Calories: 247, Fat: 13g, Carbohydrates: 4g, Protein: 6g

## Quick Turkey Cutlets

(Prepping time: 10 minutes| Cooking Time: 22 minutes |Serves: 4)

**Ingredients:**

- 1 teaspoon Greek seasoning
- 1 pound turkey cutlets
- 2 tablespoons olive oil
- 1 teaspoon turmeric powder
- ½ cup almond flour

**Preparation:**

1. Add Greek seasoning, turmeric powder, almond flour to a bowl
2. Dredge turkey cutlets in it and keep it on the side for 30 minutes
3. Set your Foodi to Saute mode and add oil and cutlets, Saute for 2 minutes
4. Lock lid and cook on LOW-MEDIUM pressure for 20 minutes
5. Quick release pressure. Serve and enjoy!

**Nutritional Information Per Serving:**

Calories: 233, Fat: 19g, Carbohydrates: 3.7g, Protein: 36g

## Pork Packed Jalapeno

(Prepping time: 10 minutes| Cooking Time: 10 minutes |Serves: 6)

**Ingredients:**

- 2 pounds pork sausage, ground
- 2 cups parmesan cheese, shredded
- 2 pounds large sized jalapeno peppers sliced lengthwise and seeded
- 2 (8 ounces packages), cream cheese, softened
- 2 (8 ounces) bottles, ranch dressing

**Preparation:**

1. Take a bowl and add pork sausage, cream cheese, ranch dressing and mix well
2. Slice jalapeno in half, remove seeds and clean them
3. Stuff sliced jalapeno pieces with pork mixture
4. Place peppers in crisping basket and transfer basket to your Ninja Foodi
5. Lock Air Crisping lid and cook on Air Crisp mode for 10 minutes at 350 degrees F
6. Cook in batches if needed, serve and enjoy!

**Nutritional Information Per Serving:**

Calories: 609, Fat: 50g, Carbohydrates: 10g, Protein: 29g

## Bacon Samba Bok Choy

(Prepping time: 10 minutes| Cooking Time:3 minutes |Serves: 4)

**Ingredients:**

- ½ tablespoons fresh lemon juice
- 1 medium ripe avocado, peeled and pitted, chopped
- 6 organic eggs, boiled, peeled and cut half
- Salt to taste
- ½ cup fresh watercress, trimmed

**Preparation:**

1. Place a steamer basket at the bottom of your Ninja Foodi
2. Add water and put watercress on the basket, lock lid and pressure cook for 3 minutes
3. Quick release pressure. Remove egg yolk and transfer to a bowl
4. Add watercress, avocado, lemon juice, salt, and mash well
5. Place egg whites in serving the dish and fill whites with watercress, mix well and enjoy!

**Nutritional Information Per Serving:**

Calories: 132, Fat: 10g, Carbohydrates: 3g, Protein: 6g

## Just A Simple Egg Frittata

(Prepping time: 10 minutes | Cooking Time: 15 minutes |Serves: 4)

**Ingredients:**

- 5 whole eggs
- ¾ teaspoon mixed herbs
- 1 cup spinach
- ¼ cup shredded cheddar cheese
- ½ cup mushrooms
- Salt and pepper to taste

¾ cup half and half

2 tablespoons butter

**Preparation:**

1. Dice mushrooms, chop spinach finely
2. Set your Ninja Foodi to Saute mode and add spinach, mushrooms
3. Whisk eggs, milk, cream cheese, herbs, and Sautéed vegetables in a bowl and mix well
4. Take a 6-inch baking pan and grease it well
5. Pour mixture and transfer to your Ninja Foodie (on a trivet)

6. Cook on HIGH pressure for 2 minutes. Quick release pressure. Serve and enjoy!

**Nutritional Information Per Serving:**

Calories: 300, Fat: 25g, Carbohydrates: 5g, Protein: 14g

# Spice Lover's Jar of Chili

(Prepping time: 10 minutes| Cooking Time: 11 minutes |Serves: 4)

**Ingredients:**

- 1 pound green chilies
- 1 and ½ cups apple cider vinegar
- 1 teaspoon pickling salt
- 1 and ½ teaspoons date paste
- ¼ teaspoon garlic powder

**Preparation:**

1. Add the above-mentioned ingredients to the Ninja Foodi
2. Lock up the lid and cook on HIGH pressure for 10 minutes
3. Release the pressure naturally
4. Spoon the mix into washed jars and cover the slices with a bit of cooking liquid
5. Add vinegar to submerge the chilly. Enjoy!

**Nutritional Information Per Serving:**

Calories: 3.1, Fat: 0g, Carbohydrates: 0.6g, Protein: 0.1g

# Everybody's Favorite Cauliflower Patties

(Prepping time: 5 minutes | Cooking Time: 20 minutes |Serves: 4)

**Ingredients:**

- 3 whole eggs
- 1 chili pepper, chopped
- ½ teaspoon garlic powder
- Salt and pepper to taste
- 2 cups cauliflower, chopped
- ¾ cups olive oil
- ¼ cup cheddar cheese
- ¼ cup whole mozzarella cheese

**Preparation:**

1. Cut cauliflower into small florets, remove leaves and cut out a core

2. Add 1 cup water to Ninja Food, transfer florets to steamer basket and place it on a trivet in your Ninja Foodi. Lock lid and cook on HIGH pressure for 5 minutes

3. Mash steamed cauliflower and dry them, add shredded cheese, eggs, chili, salt and pepper

4. Mix well and shape into flat patties

5. Heat up oil in your Ninja Foodi and set to Saute mode, shallow fry patties until crisp on both sides. Serve and enjoy!

**Nutritional Information Per Serving:**

Calories: 550, Fat: 54g, Carbohydrates: 5g, Protein: 13g

# Easy to Swallow Beet Chips

(Prepping time: 10 minutes| Cooking Time: 8 hours |For 8 servings)

**Ingredients:**

- ½ beet, peeled and cut into 1/8 inch slices

**Preparation:**

Arrange beet slices in single layer in the Cook and Crisp baske. Place the basket in the pot and close the crisping lid. Press the Dehydrate button and let it dehydrate for 8 hours at 135 degrees F. Once the dehydrating is done, remove the basket from pot and transfer slices to your Air Tight container, serve and enjoy!

**Nutritional Information Per Serving:**

Calories: 35, Fat: 0g, Carbohydrates: 8g, Protein: 1g

# Excellent Bacon and Cheddar Frittata

(Prepping time: 10 minutes| Cooking Time: 10 minutes |Serves: 6)

**Ingredients:**

- 6 whole eggs
- 2 tablespoons milk
- ½ cup bacon, cooked and chopped
- 1 cup broccoli, cooked
- ½ cup shredded cheddar cheese
- ¼ teaspoon salt
- ¼ teaspoon ground black pepper

**Preparation:**

1. Take a baking pan (small enough to fit into your Ninja Foodi) bowl, and grease it well with butter. Take a medium sized bowl and add eggs, milk, salt, pepper, bacon, broccoli, and cheese. Stir well. Pour mixture into your prepared baking pan and lower pan into your Foodi, close Air Crisping lid. Air Crisp for 7 minutes at 375 degrees F. Remove pan and enjoy!

**Nutritional Information Per Serving:**

Calories: 269, Fat: 20g, Carbohydrates: 3g, Protein: 19g

# Kale and Almonds Mix

(Prepping time: 10 minutes | Cooking Time: 4 minutes |Serves: 4)

**Ingredients:**

- 1 cup of water
- 1 big kale bunch, chopped
- 1 tablespoon balsamic vinegar
- 1/3 cup toasted almonds
- 3 garlic cloves, minced
- 1 small yellow onion, chopped
- 2 tablespoons olive oil

**Preparation:**

1. Set your Ninja Foodi on Saute mode and add oil, let it heat up
2. Stir in onion and cook for 3 minutes. Add garlic, water, kale, and stir
3. Lock lid and cook on HIGH pressure for 4 minutes. Quick release pressure
4. Add salt, pepper, vinegar, almonds and toss well. Serve and enjoy!

**Nutritional Information Per Serving:**

Calories: 140, Fat: 6g, Carbohydrates: 5g, Protein: 3g

# Veggies Dredged in Cheese

(Prepping time: 10 minutes| Cooking Time: 30 minutes |Serves: 4)

**Ingredients:**

- 2 onions, sliced
- 2 tomatoes, sliced
- 2 zucchinis, sliced
- 2 teaspoons olive oil
- 2 cups cheddar cheese, grated
- 2 teaspoons mixed dried herbs
- Salt and pepper to taste

**Preparation:**

Arrange all the listed ingredients to your Ninja Foodi. Top with olive oil, herbs, cheddar, salt and pepper. Lock lid and Air Crisp for 30 minutes at 350 degrees F. Serve and enjoy!

**Nutritional Information Per Serving:**

Calories: 305, Fat: 22g, Carbohydrates: 9g, Protein: 15g

# Chapter 7: Desserts Recipes

## Pumpkin Muffins

(Prepping time: 7 minutes| Cooking Time: 20 minutes |Serves: 5)

**Ingredients:**

- 1 tablespoon butter, melted
- 1 tablespoon pumpkin puree
- 1 teaspoon ground cinnamon
- ¼ teaspoon ground ginger
- 1 egg, beaten
- 3 tablespoon Erythritol
- ½ cup almond flour
- ½ teaspoon baking powder

**Preparation:**

1. Mix up together all the ingredients in the mixing bowl.
2. Stir the mixture well until smooth.
3. Transfer the mixture into the silicone muffin molds and place on the track in Ninja Foodi.
4. Lower the air fryer lid and set Bake mode.
5. Cook the muffins for 20 minutes at 330 F.
6. When the time is over – let the muffins rest little and serve!

**Nutritional Information Per Serving:**

calories 52, fat 4.6, fiber 0.7, carbs 8.7, protein 1.8

## Avocado Mousse

(Prepping time: 10 minutes| Cooking Time: 2 minutes |Serves: 7)

**Ingredients:**

- 2 avocado, peeled, cored
- 1 teaspoon of cocoa powder
- 1/3 cup heavy cream
- 1 teaspoon butter
- 3 tablespoons Erythritol
- 1 teaspoon vanilla extract

**Preparation:**

1. Preheat Ninja Foodi at "Sauté/Stear" mode for 5 minutes.
2. Meanwhile, mash the avocado until smooth and mix it up with Erythritol.

3. Place the butter in the pot and melt.

4. Add mashed avocado mixture and stir well.

5. Add cocoa powder and stir until homogenous. Sauté the mixture for 3 minutes.

6. Meanwhile, whisk the heavy cream on high speed for 2 minutes.

7. Transfer the cooked avocado mash in the bowl and chill in ice water.

8. When the avocado mash reaches room temperature – add whisked heavy cream and vanilla extract. Stir gently to get white-chocolate swirls.

9. Transfer the mousse into small cups and chill for 4 hours in the fridge.

10. Serve!

**Nutritional Information Per Serving:**

calories 144, fat 13.9, fiber 3.9, carbs 10.5, protein 1.3

# Keto Donuts

(Prepping time: 20 minutes| Cooking Time: 10 minutes |Serves: 5)

**Ingredients:**

- 1 ½ cup almond flour
- ½ teaspoon baking soda
- 1 teaspoon vanilla extract
- 1 egg, whisked
- 2 tablespoons Erythritol
- ½ cup heavy cream

**Preparation:**

1. Mix up together the whisked egg, heavy cream, Erythritol, vanilla extract, and baking soda.

2. When the mixture is homogenous – add almond flour. Stir well and knead the non-sticky dough.

3. Let the dough rest for 10 minutes.

4. After this, roll up the dough with the help of the rolling pin into 1 inch thick.

5. Then make the donuts with the help of the cutter.

6. Set the Ninja Foodi Bake mode + Roast option and set 360 F.

7. When the appliance is preheated – place the donuts in the basket and lower the air fryer lid.

8. Cook the donuts for 5 minutes.

9. Chill the donuts well and serve!

**Nutritional Information Per Serving:**

calories 118, fat 11.5, fiber 1, carbs 2.4, protein 2.7

# Peanut Butter Cookies

(Prepping time: 10 minutes| Cooking Time: 11 minutes |Serves: 7)

**Ingredients:**

- 1 tablespoon Truvia
- 1 egg, whisked
- 6 oz cashew butter

**Preparation:**

1. Mix up together all the ingredients and make the small balls.
2. Place the balls in the basket of Ninja Foodi and close the lid.
3. Set the Bake mode and cook the cookies at 330 F for 11 minutes.
4. Increase the time of cooking if you like crunchy cookies.
5. Serve!

**Nutritional Information Per Serving:**

calories 152, fat 12.6, fiber 0.5, carbs 7.4, protein 5.1

# Raspberry Dump Cake

(Prepping time: 10 minutes| Cooking Time: 30 minutes |Serves: 10)

**Ingredients:**

- 1 ½ cup coconut flour
- 1 teaspoon baking powder
- 1 teaspoon lemon juice
- ½ cup raspberries
- ¼ cup Erythritol
- 1 egg, whisked
- 1/3 cup almond milk
- 1 tablespoon butter, melted
- ½ teaspoon vanilla extract

**Preparation:**

1. Combine together all the dry ingredients.
2. Then add egg, almond milk, and butter.
3. Add vanilla extract and lemon juice.
4. Stir the mixture well. You have to get a liquid batter.
5. Place the layer of the raspberries in the silicone mold.
6. Pour batter over the raspberries.
7. Place the mold on the rack and insert it into Ninja Foodi basket.

8. Close the air fryer lid and set Bake mode.

9. Cook the cake for 30 minutes at 350 F.

10. When the cake is cooked – chill it well.

11. Turn upside down and transfer on the serving plate.

12. Enjoy!

**Nutritional Information Per Serving:**

calories 107, fat 4.5, fiber 8.9, carbs 15.1, protein 4.3

# Vanilla Muffins

(Prepping time: 7 minutes| Cooking Time: 2 minutes |Serves: 4)

**Ingredients:**

- 4 tablespoon coconut flour
- 1 teaspoon coconut shred
- 1 teaspoon vanilla extract
- 1 egg, beaten
- 1 tablespoon Truvia
- ¼ teaspoon baking powder
- 1 cup water, for cooking

**Preparation:**

1. Mix up together all the ingredients and stir well until you get a thick batter.

2. Add water in the Ninja Foodi basket.

3. Place the batter into the muffin molds and transfer them on the Ninja Foodi rack.

4. Lower the pressure cooker lid and set Pressure mode (High pressure).

5. Cook the muffins for 2 minutes. Use the quick pressure release method.

6. Chill the muffins and serve!

**Nutritional Information Per Serving:**

calories 61, fat 2.9, fiber 3.3, carbs 7, protein 2.5

# Blackberry Cake

(Prepping time: 8 minutes| Cooking Time: 25 minutes |Serves: 4)

**Ingredients:**

- 4 tablespoons butter
- 3 tablespoon Erythritol
- 2 eggs, whisked
- ½ teaspoon vanilla extract
- 1 oz blackberries

- 1 cup almond flour
- ½ teaspoon baking powder

**Preparation:**

1.  Combine together all the liquid ingredients.
2.  Then add baking powder, almond flour, and Erythritol.
3.  Stir the mixture until smooth.
4.  Add blackberries and stir the batter gently with the help of the spoon.
5.  Take the non-sticky springform pan and transfer the batter inside.
6.  Place the springform pan in the pot and lower the air fryer lid.
7.  Cook the cake for 20 minutes at 365 F.
8.  When the time is over – check the doneness of the cake with the help of the toothpick and cook for 5 minutes more if needed.
9.  Chill it little and serve!

**Nutritional Information Per Serving:**

calories 173, fat 16.7, fiber 1.1, carbs 2.2, protein 4.2

# Lava Cups

(Prepping time: 6 minutes| Cooking Time: 8 minutes |Serves: 2)

**Ingredients:**

- 2 eggs, whisked
- 3 tablespoons flax meal
- 2 teaspoon of cocoa powder
- ½ teaspoon baking powder
- 2 tablespoons heavy cream
- Cooking spray

**Preparation:**

1.  Spray the cake cups with the cooking spray inside.
2.  Mix up together all the remaining ingredients and pour the mixture into the prepared cups.
3.  Cover the cups with foil and place in Ninja Foodi.
4.  Set the Bake mode 355 F.
5.  Close the lid and cook the dessert for 8 minutes.
6.  Serve the cooked lava cups hot!

**Nutritional Information Per Serving:**

calories 165, fat 13.9, fiber 3.6, carbs 5.3, protein 8.4

# Keto Brownie

(Prepping time: 10 minutes| Cooking Time: 32 minutes |Serves: 6)

**Ingredients:**

* 3 tablespoons Truvia
* 1 oz sugar-free chocolate chips
* 2 eggs, whisked
* ½ teaspoon vanilla extract
* 3 tablespoon butter, melted
* 1 tablespoon almond flour

**Preparation:**

1. Whisk together the melted butter, almond flour, vanilla extract, and Truvia.
2. Melt the chocolate chips and add them in the butter mixture.
3. Add eggs and stir until smooth.
4. Pour the batter into Ninja Foodi basket (Bake mode) and cook at 360 F for 32 minutes.
5. Then check if the brownie cooked and chill well.
6. Cut it into the servings and serve!

**Nutritional Information Per Serving:**

calories 99, fat 8.8, fiber 0.1, carbs 5.9, protein 2.4

# Ginger Cookies

(Prepping time: 10 minutes| Cooking Time: 14 minutes |Serves: 7)

**Ingredients:**

* 1 cup almond flour
* 3 tablespoons butter
* 1 egg
* ½ teaspoon baking powder
* 3 tablespoon Erythritol
* 1 teaspoon ground ginger
* ½ teaspoon ground cinnamon
* 3 tablespoons heavy cream

**Preparation:**

1. Beat the egg in the bowl and whisk it gently.
2. Add baking powder, Erythritol, ground ginger, ground cinnamon, heavy cream, and flour.
3. Stir gently and add butter,
4. Knead the non-sticky dough.

5.  Roll up the dough with the help of the rolling pin and make the cookies with the help of the cutter.

6.  Place the cookies in the basket in one layer and close the lid.

7.  Set the Bake mode and cook the cookies for 14 minutes at 350 F.

8.  When the cookies are cooked – let them chill well and serve!

**Nutritional Information Per Serving:**

calories 172, fat 15.6, fiber 1.8, carbs 4.1, protein 4.4


# Vanilla Custard

(Prepping time: 5 minutes| Cooking Time: 10 minutes |Serves: 4)

**Ingredients:**

*   3 egg yolks

*   1 cup almond milk

*   1 teaspoon vanilla extract

*   2 tablespoon Truvia

**Preparation:**

1.  Whisk together egg yolk and Truvia.

2.  Add vanilla extract and almond milk.

3.  Preheat Ninja Foodi at Sauté/Stear mode at 365F for 5 minutes

4.  Then pour the almond milk mixture and Sauté it for 10 minutes.

5.  Stir the liquid all the time.

6.  When the liquid start to be thick – transfer it into the serving jars and leave it for 1 hour in the fridge.

7.  Serve it!

**Nutritional Information Per Serving:**

calories 181, fat 17.7, fiber 1.3, carbs 6.2, protein 3.4


# Mini Cheesecakes

(Prepping time: 30 minutes| Cooking Time: 4 minutes |Serves: 4)

**Ingredients:**

*   8 tablespoons cream cheese

*   4 tablespoon Erythritol

*   2 tablespoons heavy cream

*   ½ teaspoon vanilla extract

*   4 tablespoons almond flour

**Preparation:**

1. Whisk together the cream cheese and heavy cream.
2. When the mixture is smooth – add 1 tablespoon of Erythritol and stir until homogenous.
3. After this, add vanilla extract and stir again.
4. Scoop the medium balls from the cream cheese mixture.
5. Mix up together the almond flour and all the remaining Erythritol.
6. Then coat every cheesecake ball into the almond flour mixture.
7. Freeze the balls for 20 minutes or until they are solid.
8. Place the cheesecake balls in the Ninja Foodi basket and lower the air fryer lid.
9. Cook the dessert at 400 F for 4 minutes.
10. When the time is over – serve the dessert immediately.
11. Taste it!

**Nutritional Information Per Serving:**

calories 139, fat 13.1, fiber 0.8, carbs 2.3, protein 3.2

# Chip Cookies

(Prepping time: 10 minutes| Cooking Time: 9 minutes |Serves: 8)

**Ingredients:**

- 1 oz sugar-free chocolate chips
- 3 tablespoon butter
- 1 cup almond flour
- 1 egg, whisked
- 2 tablespoons Erythritol

**Preparation:**

1. Mix up together the almond flour and whisked the egg.
2. Add butter and Erythritol, and mix up the mixture until homogenous.
3. Add chocolate chips and knead the homogenous dough.
4. Make 8 small balls from the dough and transfer them on the rack of Ninja Foodi.
5. Close the air fryer lid and set Bake mode.
6. Cook the chip cookies for 9 minutes at 360 F.
7. Chill the cookies and serve!

**Nutritional Information Per Serving:**

calories 145, fat 12.3, fiber 1.5, carbs 8.4, protein 3.9

# Vanilla Creme Brulee

(Prepping time: 20 minutes| Cooking Time: 10 minutes |Serves: 3)

## Ingredients:

- 1 cup heavy cream
- 4 egg yolks
- 3 tablespoons Truvia
- ½ teaspoon vanilla extract

## Preparation:

1. Whisk together the egg yolks and 2 tablespoons of Truvia.
2. Add heavy cream and stir until homogenous.
3. Place the mixture into the ramekins and cover them with the foil.
4. Make the small holes on the top of the foil with the help of the toothpick.
5. Pour ½ cup of water in Ninja Foofi basket and insert trivet.
6. Place the ramekins on the trivet and close the pressure cooker lid.
7. Cook the dessert on Pressure mode (High pressure) for 10 minutes.
8. Then make the quick pressure release for 5 minutes.
9. Let the dessert chill for 10 minutes.
10. Remove the foil from the ramekins and sprinkle the surface of creme brulee with Truvia.
11. Use the hand torch to caramelize the surface.
12. Serve it!

## Nutritional Information Per Serving:

calories 212, fat 20.8, fiber 0, carbs 6.7, protein 4.4

# Cinnamon Bites

(Prepping time: 10 minutes| Cooking Time: 12 minutes |Serves: 5)

## Ingredients:

- 1 teaspoon ground cinnamon
- 1 cup almond flour
- ½ teaspoon baking powder
- 1 teaspoon olive oil
- ¼ cup almond milk
- 1 teaspoon butter
- ½ teaspoon vanilla extract
- 1 cup water, for cooking

## Preparation:

1. Combine together all the dry ingredients.

2. Then add butter and almond milk in the dry ingredients.

3. Add vanilla extract and olive oil and knead the smooth and non-sticky dough.

4. Make the medium balls from the dough and place them in the silicone molds.

5. Pour water in Ninja Foodi basket.

6. Place the molds on the rack in Ninja Foodi.

7. Close the lid and seal it.

8. Set Pressure mode (High pressure)

9. Cook the cinnamon bites for 10 minutes.

10. Then make natural pressure release for 10 minutes.

11. Then remove the liquid from the basket and lower the air fryer lid.

12. Set Air Crisp and cook the bites for 2 minutes more.

13. Serve!

**Nutritional Information Per Serving:**

calories 180, fat 15.2, fiber 2.9, carbs 6.1, protein 5.1

# Keto Brownie Batter

(Prepping time: 10 minutes| Cooking Time: 5 minutes |Serves: 5)

**Ingredients:**

- 1/3 cup almond flour
- 1 tablespoon Erythritol
- ¼ cup heavy cream
- ½ teaspoon vanilla extract
- 3 tablespoons cocoa powder
- 3 tablespoons butter
- 1 oz dark chocolate

**Preparation:**

1. Place the almond flour in the springform pan and flatten to make the layer.

2. Then place the springform pan in the pot and lower the air fryer lid.

3. Cook the almond flour for 3 minutes at 400 F or until the almond flour gets a golden color.

4. Meanwhile, combine together cocoa powder and heavy cream; whisk the heavy cream until smooth.

5. Add vanilla extract and Erythritol.

6. Remove the almond flour from Ninja Foodi and chill well.

7. Toss butter and dark chocolate in the pot and preheat for 1 minute on Sauté/Stear mode.

8. When the butter is soft – add it in the heavy cream mixture.

9. Then add chocolate and almond flour.

10. Stir the mass until homogenous and serve!

**Nutritional Information Per Serving:**

calories 159, fat 14.9, fiber 2.1, carbs 9, protein 2.5

# Coconut Pie

(Prepping time: 6 minutes| Cooking Time: 10 minutes |Serves: 4)

**Ingredients:**

- 1 tablespoon coconut flour
- 5 oz coconut, shredded
- ½ teaspoon vanilla extract
- 1 tablespoon Truvia
- 1 teaspoon butter
- 1 egg, whisked
- ¼ cup heavy cream

**Preparation:**

1. Mix up together the coconut flour, coconut shred, and butter.
2. Stir the mixture until homogenous.
3. Add whisked egg, vanilla extract, Truvia, and heavy cream. Stir well.
4. Transfer the pie mixture into the basket and lower the air fryer lid.
5. Set the Bake mode 355F.
6. Cook the pie for 10 minutes.
7. Check if the pie is cooked with the help of the toothpick and chill it till the room temperature.
8. Serve it!

**Nutritional Information Per Serving:**

calories 185, fat 16.9, fiber 3.9, carbs 8.2, protein 3

# Sweet Zucchini Crisp

(Prepping time: 5 minutes| Cooking Time: 10 minutes |Serves: 4)

**Ingredients:**

- 1 zucchini, chopped
- 1 teaspoon Vanilla extract
- 2 tablespoon Erythritol
- 1 tablespoon coconut flakes
- 2 tablespoon butter
- 1 tablespoon almond flour

**Preparation:**

1. Preheat Ninja Foodi at Sauté/Stear mode for 5 minutes at 360 F.

2. Toss the butter in the Ninja Foodi basket.

3. Add chopped zucchini and Sauté the vegetables for 3 minutes.

4. Add vanilla extract, coconut flakes, Erythritol, and stir well.

5. Cook the zucchini for 4 minutes more.

6. Then add almond flour and stir well.

7. Sauté the dessert for 1 minute.

8. Use the Air crips mode for 2 minutes to get a crunchy crust.

9. Serve the cooked dessert immediately!

**Nutritional Information Per Serving:**

calories 84, fat 8.5, fiber 0.5, carbs 6.1, protein 0.3

# Mint Cake

(Prepping time: 8 minutes| Cooking Time: 62 minutes |Serves: 6)

**Ingredients:**

- 1 teaspoon dried mint
- 1 cup coconut flour
- 1 teaspoon baking powder
- ¼ cup Erythritol
- 2 eggs, whisked
- ¼ cup heavy cream
- 1 tablespoon butter
- ½ teaspoon lemon zest, grated

**Preparation:**

1. In the mixing bowl mix up together all the ingredients.

2. Use the cooking machine to make the soft batter from the mixture.

3. Pour the batter in the Ninja Foodie basket and flatten it well.

4. Close the pressure cooker lid and set Pressure mode. Seal the lid.

5. Cook the cake on Low pressure for 55 minutes.

6. Then lower the air fryer lid and set Air Crisp mode.

7. Cook the cake for 7 minutes more at 400 F.

8. Chill the cake well and serve!

**Nutritional Information Per Serving:**

calories 136, fat 7.2, fiber 8.1, carbs 22, protein 4.7

# Cinnamon Bun

(Prepping time: 10 minutes| Cooking Time: 15 minutes |Serves: 8)

**Ingredients:**

- 1 cup almond flour
- ½ teaspoon baking powder
- 3 tablespoon Erythritol
- 2 tablespoon ground cinnamon
- ½ teaspoon vanilla extract
- 1 tablespoon butter
- 1 egg, whisked
- ¾ teaspoon salt
- ¼ cup almond milk

**Preparation:**

1. Mix up together the almond flour, baking powder, vanilla extract, egg, salt, and almond milk.
2. Knead the soft and non-sticky dough.
3. Roll up the dough with the help of the rolling pin.
4. Sprinkle dough with the butter, cinnamon, and Erythritol.
5. Roll the dough into the log.
6. Cut the roll into 7 pieces.
7. Spray Ninja Foodi basket with the cooking spray.
8. Place the cinnamon buns in the basket and close the lid.
9. Set the Bake mode and cook the buns for 15 minutes at 355 F.
10. Check if the buns are cooked with the help of the toothpick.
11. Chill the buns well and serve!

**Nutritional Information Per Serving:**

calories 127, fat 10.5, fiber 3, carbs 9.2, protein 4


# Pumpkin Pie

(Prepping time: 10 minutes| Cooking Time: 25 minutes |Serves: 6)

**Ingredients:**

- 1 tablespoon pumpkin puree
- 1 cup coconut flour
- ½ teaspoon baking powder
- 1 teaspoon apple cider vinegar
- 1 teaspoon Pumpkin spices

- 1 tablespoon butter
- ¼ cup heavy cream
- 2 tablespoon liquid stevia
- 1 egg, whisked

**Preparation:**

1. Melt the butter and combine it together with the heavy cream, apple cider vinegar, liquid stevia, egg, and baking powder.

2. Add pumpkin puree and coconut flour.

3. After this, add pumpkin spices and stir the batter until smooth.

4. Pour the batter in Ninja Foodi basket and lower the air fryer lid.

5. Set the "Bake" mode 360 F.

6. Cook the pie for 25 minutes.

7. When the time is over – let the pie chill till the room temperature. Serve it!

**Nutritional Information Per Serving:**

calories 127, fat 6.6, fiber 8.1, carbs 14.2, protein 3.8


# Pecan Muffins

(Prepping time: 10 minutes| Cooking Time: 12 minutes |Serves: 6)

**Ingredients:**

- 4 tablespoon butter, softened
- 4 tablespoon coconut flour
- 1 egg, whisked
- 4 tablespoon heavy cream
- ½ teaspoon vanilla extract
- 1 tablespoon pecans, crushed
- 2 tablespoon Erythritol

**Preparation:**

1. In the mixing bowl combine together the coconut flour, softened butter, whisked egg, heavy cream, vanilla extract, and Erythritol.

2. Use the hand mixer to mix up the mixture until smooth.

3. Pour the smooth batter in the silicone muffin molds.

4. Top every muffin with the pecans and transfer in Ninja Foodi rack.

5. Lower the air fryer lid and set Bake mode.

6. Cook the muffins for 12 minutes at 350 F.

7. Check if the muffins are cooked and transfer on the plate. Chill well and serve!

**Nutritional Information Per Serving:**

calories 170, fat 15.1, fiber 3.6, carbs 11.1, protein 2.8

# Tender Pudding

(Prepping time: 10 minutes| Cooking Time: 25 minutes |Serves: 4)

## Ingredients:

- 3 eggs, whisked
- ½ teaspoon vanilla extract
- 4 tablespoons pumpkin puree
- 1 teaspoon pumpkin pie spices
- 1 cup heavy cream
- 2 tablespoon Erythritol
- 1 cup water, for cooking

## Preparation:

1. Whisk together the eggs, vanilla extract, pumpkin puree, pumpkin pie spices, cream, and Erythritol.

2. Pour the liquid into the non-sticky cake pan.

3. Pour water in the pot.

4. Place the pudding in a cake pan in the pot on the rack and close the lid.

5. Select Steam mode and cook the dessert for 25 minutes.

6. Let the cooked pudding rest for 10 minutes (open Foodi lid).

7. Place it in the fridge for a minimum of 4 hours.

8. Enjoy!

## Nutritional Information Per Serving:

calories 159, fat 14.5, fiber 0.5, carbs 2.7, protein 5

# Chocolate Cakes

(Prepping time: 10 minutes| Cooking Time: 22 minutes |Serves: 3)

**Ingredients:**

- 1 tablespoon cocoa powder
- 4 tablespoons almond flour
- ½ teaspoon vanilla extract
- 1 tablespoon Truvia
- 1/3 cup heavy cream
- ¼ teaspoon baking powder
- Cooking spray

**Preparation:**

1. Mix up together the cocoa powder, almond flour, vanilla extract, Truvia, heavy cream, and baking powder.
2. Use the mixer to make the smooth batter.
3. Spray the silicone molds with the cooking spray inside.
4. Pour the batter into the silicone molds and transfer then in Ninja Foodi basket.
5. Close the air fryer lid and set Bake-Roast Option.
6. Cook the cakes at 255 F for 22 minutes.
7. Serve the dessert chilled!

**Nutritional Information Per Serving:**

calories 108, fat 9.6, fiber 1.6, carbs 5.2, protein 2.6

# Almond Bites

(Prepping time: 10 minutes| Cooking Time: 14 minutes |Serves: 5)

**Ingredients:**

- 1 egg, whisked
- 1 cup almond flour
- ¼ cup almond milk
- 1 tablespoon coconut flakes
- ½ teaspoon vanilla extract
- ½ teaspoon baking powder
- ½ teaspoon apple cider vinegar
- 2 tablespoons butter

**Preparation:**

1. Mix up together the whisked egg, almond milk, apple cider vinegar, baking powder, vanilla extract, and butter.
2. Stir the mixture and add almond flour and coconut flakes. Knead the dough.
3. If the dough is sticky – add more almond flour.
4. Make the medium balls from the dough and place them on the rack of Ninja Foodi.
5. Press them gently with the hand palm.
6. Lower the air fryer lid and cook the dessert for 12 minutes at 360 F.
7. Check if the dessert is cooked – and cook for 2 minutes more for a crunchy crust.
8. Enjoy!

**Nutritional Information Per Serving:**

calories 118, fat 11.5, fiber 1, carbs 2.4, protein 2.7

CPSIA information can be obtained
at www.ICGtesting.com
Printed in the USA
BVHW052205130222
628955BV00002B/86